101 BIKE ROUTES IN SCOTLAND

101 Bike Routes in Scotland

Harry Henniker

MAINSTREAM
PUBLISHING
EDINBURGH AND LONDON

Revised and updated, 2004
Copyright © Harry Henniker, 1996
All rights reserved

The moral right of the author has been asserted

First published in Great Britain in 1996 by
MAINSTREAM PUBLISHING COMPANY (EDINBURGH) LTD
7 Albany Street
Edinburgh EH1 3UG

ISBN 1 84018 834 X

A catalogue record for this book is available from the British Library.

Maps drawn by the author using a vector graphics drawing package. Maps
manually re-drawn from out-of-copyright editions of the Ordnance Survey One
Inch Map supplied in photocopied form by the National Library of Scotland and
updated by direct observation and with Garmin GPS software. Heights on maps
taken with a Thommen Altimeter.

Typeset in Janson Text and Gill Sans
Printed by The Bath Press Ltd

CONTENTS

Shetland
Islands

Orkney Islands

Outer Hebrides

Western Isles

Northern Highlands

Skye

Central
Highlands

Isle of
Mull

Jura

Glasgow

Edinburgh

Islay

Arran

South Scotland

England

INTRODUCTION

This is a book mostly about cycling on quiet minor roads, cyclepaths, canal towpaths and the like. While mountain bikes are perfectly good for this, they aren't really necessary most of the time. There are a few routes which take in some easy forest roads and this will be indicated. Technically difficult mountain bike routes are avoided.

This book was originally published in 1996 and, unfortunately, there has been a considerable increase in motor traffic since then. This has meant that some of the routes in the original book are now less pleasant, so these have been taken out. On the other hand, the National Cycle Network is now around 2,000 miles long in Scotland and much of that is on specially built cyclepaths, converted railway lines, etc., so it's not all bad news. Sustrans and the National Cycle Network deserve your support.

Some routes in this book occasionally follow scenic parts of the National Cycle Network and other cycle routes signposted by local authorities. These other routes are all perfectly fine but they are sometimes designed for different purposes: for example, to attract tourists to a particular area; to provide useful commuter routes for cyclists; to be part of some urban regeneration scheme. Personally, if I'm cycling for fun, I'll avoid the shopping malls and head for the beautiful scenery. Routes in this book try to avoid urban areas. If you see signs for other bike routes, don't assume that they are the same routes as in this book – they may not be!

MAPS

The instructions and the maps in this book should be enough to enable you to find your way. Bear in mind, of course, that they only show the immediate area. It's best to have a general map as well, and Ordnance Survey (OS) maps are the best ones to get. The OS Road Map series (1:250,000) should be sufficient, and these cover Scotland in three sheets. The OS also publish the 1:50,000 Landranger series. These are great for showing you the way in detail; 85 maps are necessary to cover the whole of Scotland. All of these maps are contour (topographical) maps.

MAP SYMBOLS

The map symbols in this book are indicated on each individual map; north is always at the top of the map. The cycle route is highlighted in red. Where the route is circular, i.e. starting and finishing at the same point, the arrows will be solid red. Where the route is not circular, i.e. part of a long distance route or you have to return the way you went out, the arrows will be in outline.

circular ➔   not circular ⇒

ROUTE GRADING

Easy – fairly easy cycling, some hills but they will not be very steep and long.

Varied – varied cycling with some hills, either steep but short, or longer but easier.

Hilly – serious hills that are sufficiently frequent that getting off and walking is not really an option. Low gears and being fit is the only answer!

OFF-ROAD GRADING

The above grades describe how hilly the route is. If the route has some sections away from tarmac surfaces and public roads, these will be graded as follows:

Any bike – canal towpath, easy forest road, or converted railway line, may be good for children.

Mountain bike – forest roads, Land Rover tracks, narrow paths, rough or muddy in places. Mountain bikes are not essential but those with narrow tyres, or cyclists with little experience, may sometimes need to walk.

ACKNOWLEDGEMENTS

My first acknowledgement must be to members, past and present, of Spokes, the Lothian Cycle Campaign. As well as campaigning for better facilities for cyclists around Edinburgh and throughout Scotland, members have, over the years, cycled in many of the best places in Scotland. To a large extent, it is their explorations that I have drawn on while writing this book.

I would like to thank Peter Hawkins for his help in checking out routes in the north of Scotland, and Dave McArthur, my companion for many a mile, for his help with off-road routes. A few parts of the routes in this book follow sections of the National Cycle Network and I would like to thank everyone in the Scottish office of Sustrans, and Tony Grant in particular, for help with this.

I should also thank Elaine Abbot for help with Islay and Jura, and my brother Dave for sorting out occasional computer problems. Thanks are also due to many other cyclists who have suggested good places to ride a bike.

Visit Scotland doesn't always get a good press but I have found them unfailingly helpful. Often tourism professionals are cyclists themselves and they have detailed knowledge of bike routes in their own area. In particular, I should thank Gavin Walls for his help with the Orkney Islands and Linda Galt for help with the Appendix.

SOUTH SCOTLAND

DISTANCES AND ROUTE GRADING

CHAPTER 1

SOUTH SCOTLAND

As you'll see from page 13, this book is organised as a series of mostly circular routes. These can be linked up to provide longer tours, such as the coast to coast route in this section from Stranraer in the west, to Dunbar or Berwick-upon-Tweed in the east. Berwick-upon-Tweed was once part of Scotland but the English took it over in 1482.

The routes are generally on quiet minor roads, although there are a few off-road sections following forest tracks and the like. Generally these will be rideable on any bicycle, although you may prefer to walk on a few rough footpath sections.

South Scotland is an area with a wide choice of minor roads, many of which carry very little traffic. This is particularly so in Dumfries and Galloway. You might only see one car every half-hour on some roads. The Borders are a little busier. Galashiels and Melrose are becoming popular with commuters to Edinburgh, so class A roads should be avoided here. Some of the routes in this book follow minor roads that are signed as cycle routes by local authorities, for example the National Cycle Network or the Borderloop. National Cycle Network routes are indicated – otherwise ignore other cycle route signs.

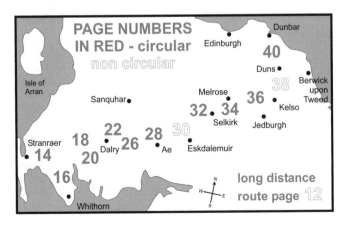

STRANRAER TO DUNBAR LONG DISTANCE ROUTE

A 224-mile coast to coast by the forests, hills and rivers of south Scotland
Route grading: **Varied** (224 miles)

This long distance route is on quiet minor roads with lots of historic interest. There are castles and great houses, cosy pubs, friendly tearooms.

As you can see from the map, this route can be done as a long distance coast to coast route, or as a series of circular day rides. For detailed descriptions of each section, see the following pages. Each ride has a map. There is detailed information about how hilly the route is, distances, refreshment stops, and what there is to see.

Virtually all the route is on quiet minor roads. Cars should not be a problem – a few roads are so quiet you may hardly see any cars at all. If you are arriving by train, check out train times and reserve a place on the train for your bike in advance. There are train stations at Stranraer, Sanquhar, Dunbar and Berwick-upon-Tweed.

If you are staying overnight, there is a wide choice of accommodation, from youth hostels and campsites, to B&Bs and hotels. The small towns each have their own individual character and aren't particularly touristy.

There are very many places of historic and natural interest in the south of Scotland. Whithorn is the place where Scotland first started to become a Christian country in the fifth century and if you cycle through there you'll be able to see round the remains of the historic priory.

Quite near here too is Galloway Forest Park, a huge area with lots of wildlife: red deer, pine marten and wild goats, to name a few. Recently the area has been developed for mountain biking and there are lots of interesting trails for all abilities. If you are doing the long distance route, it is possible to include a number of long off-road sections to make things more challenging!

Between Melrose and Berwick-upon-Tweed the route uses the Tweed Cycleway and National Cycle Network Route 1 to travel through the Scottish Borders. Along the way, there are circular routes to explore the rivers and valleys, and the great abbeys and castles. Gradients are usually gentle in the valleys but crossing between them will involve a climb.

Sheep farming is important here and if you are cycling for more than a day or two, you are certain to see the familiar black and white border collie, still a working dog in this area. The border forests are quite extensive too. Glentress, Cardrona and Elibank and Traquair Forests have a number of off-road bike routes. You could take in some of these in the coast to coast.

All the border towns are attractive but Kelso is particularly so, with its elegant town square and beautiful ruined abbey. After Kelso, you can either strike north to catch a train home from Dunbar, or briefly enter England to go home from Berwick-upon-Tweed.

If you elect for the northern option, you'll pass through Abbey St Bathans, with its ancient oak woods and the remains of its twelfth-century priory. There are some lung-bursting hills here too, but if you've come from Stranraer, you'll be sufficiently fit by now that they won't cause you any problem.

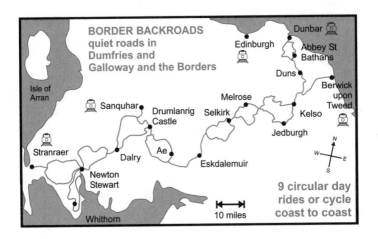

NEWTON STEWART TO GLENLUCE

A scenic circular, forests, coastal scenery
Route grading: **Varied** (47 miles)
Linking section from Stranraer: **Hilly** (15 miles)

Turn left off the A714 north of Newton Stewart and climb through trees. There is a downhill then you pass two lochs on the left. Turn left at a stone bridge to cross the River Bladnoch. After this, you climb gently for five miles. Keep straight on at the next junction. You pass a caravan park, ignore the right turn for New Luce unless you are going to Stranraer.

Glenluce Abbey (a ruin) is worth seeing. Near too is the Castle of Park, which has been restored. Glenluce has hotels and shops, a good place for a lunch break.

Cross the A75, taking the minor road opposite the junction on the west side of Glenluce. At Glen of Luce, you join the A747 for three miles, turn left off it on to the B7005. After this, the route back to Newton Stewart is a lovely ride, with the hills of Cairnsmore of Fleet forming a scenic backdrop. Turn off the A75 to the minor road on the map to avoid the roundabout at the A714 Junction.

Linking section from Stranraer
Leave Stranraer on the A75. After passing a school with playing fields, turn right at a sign: 'Industrial estate'. After 200 metres, turn left (no sign). After this, follow Southern Upland Way signs (thistle symbol on post). Turn left under a rail bridge at a T junction. After the bridge, follow the thistle symbols to Castle Kennedy, passing through a wood then through Castle Kennedy village to Castle Kennedy. Take care crossing the A75.

Go through the castle grounds, following the signs. Keep on tarmac to a coach park, then turn right to a dirt track. Turn left at the road. In the opposite direction, you will see Cults Loch just before this entry point. Continue along the minor road for five miles to New Luce. This is a pretty village with a pub and shop. Turn right in New Luce, then first left after the pub to continue to Tarf Bridge.

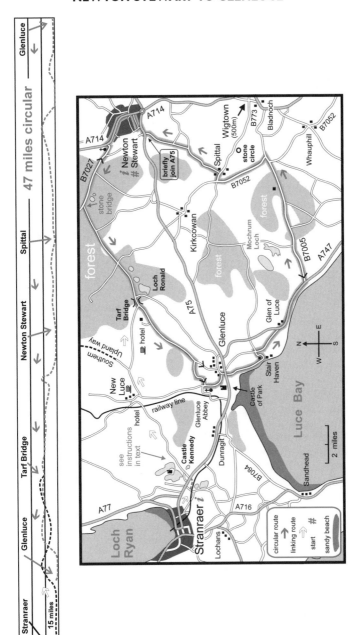

NEWTON STEWART TO ISLE OF WHITHORN

Rolling scenery with views of the sea and hills
Route grading: **Easy** (22, 33 or 51 miles)

This route is a figure of eight with three options: a Newton Stewart to Wigtown circular route of 22 miles; a Wigtown to Isle of Whithorn circle of 33 miles; or a combined route of 51 miles. The countryside around here is very quiet, with lots of dairy farms.

From Newton Stewart, cross the A75 to the A714. Continue south for over a mile then turn left at a phone box signed 'Moss of Cree'. After that, the route is as on the map. Before Wigtown, you pass the Martyr's Stake where Margaret Wilson was drowned by the tide for refusing to renounce her religion. Wigtown has tearooms and second-hand bookshops. Garlieston has an interesting sleepy harbour, and the Harbour Inn does bar lunches.

Despite its name, the Isle of Whithorn is part of the mainland. It is joined by Harbour Row. There's a great pub called the Steam Packet Inn, which does bar lunches, and a little harbour with fishing boats and yachts. Nearby too is St Ninian's Chapel, the ruin of a thirteenth-century chapel on a site traditionally associated with St Ninian. It's by the sea, a great spot for a picnic, with wild flowers and views over Wigtown Bay. Five miles further along the route, an interesting diversion is to St Ninian's Cave, a short walk by a stream to a wild pebble beach. St Ninian liked coming here, and when you see it you'll understand why.

Whithorn has a choice of tearooms and pubs, as well as a visitor centre which includes an archaeological dig and museum. St Ninian's mission here began in 397 AD, nearly two centuries before St Columba arrived from Ireland and started the Celtic church in Iona further north. St Ninian was born and educated under the Roman Empire, which still existed at this time.

Cycling back to Newton Stewart or Wigtown, note that there are no sources of food, so take something with you.

NEWTON STEWART TO ISLE OF WHITHORN

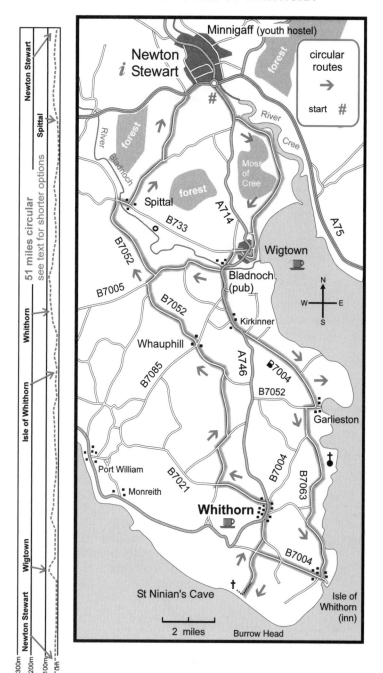

NEWTON STEWART TO CLATTERINGSHAWS

A very scenic circular route (part off-road)
Route grading: **Hilly – mountain bike** (41 miles)

This would be unsuitable for bikes with narrow tyres or if you are carrying a lot of luggage. Partly it's National Cycle Network Route 7. In Newton Stewart, bike over the bridge to Minnigaff. Cycle past the youth hostel (old school) and turn left (north). The road winds past a church and along the east bank of the River Cree.

After three miles, it passes the Wood of Cree bird reserve. Turn right half a mile after the Water of Trool, then turn right at a T junction by the Water of Minnoch. There's a visitor centre here with a tearoom. Two miles after this, just before Loch Trool, there is a right turn giving access to a Forestry Commission campsite. The Glen Trool road climbs steeply, ending at the Bruce's Stone commemorating Robert the Bruce's first victory. The view is pretty good too, and you can see the next section of the route, which is off-road.

Continue down a steeply plunging dirt track, crossing two bridges and cattle grids to enter oak woods. A forest road takes you across the Glenhead Burn. Turn left to continue east at the T junction. There is a climb then a descent to Loch Dee. Pass Loch Dee and White Laggan Bothy (rough shelter). You can stay there for nothing but you need a sleeping bag, stove, etc.

A point that needs care here is to look out for the left turn crossing the River Dee. You'll be flying downhill at that point. When you get to the A712, turn right. After a mile, you pass Clatteringshaws Visitor Centre (tearoom). You can return to Newton Stewart on the A712; this is fairly quiet but you could avoid most of it by using the Old Edinburgh Road (entry at Black Loch car park) and the minor roads near Minnigaff (see map). These are both prettier and quieter than the A712. The Old Edinburgh Road is a forest dirt road.

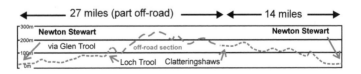

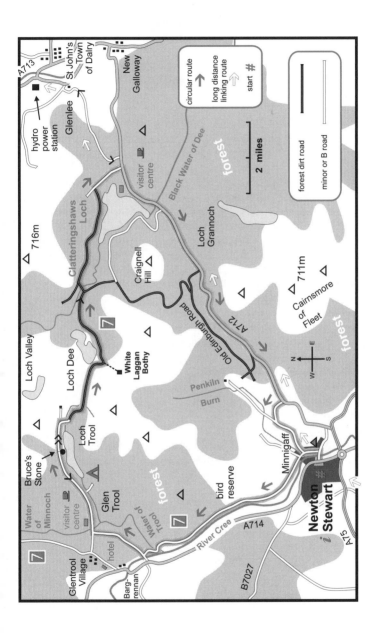

NEWTON STEWART TO DALRY

Route all by public road
Route grading: **Varied** (22 miles)
(Dalry is also known as St John's Town of Dalry)

This description is provided for those doing the coast to coast who do not want to have an off-road section. Part of the route is on the A712, but this is reasonably quiet despite being a class A road.

In Newton Stewart, cycle over the bridge to Minnigaff. Cycle past the youth hostel (in an old school) and keep straight on at this point (i.e. don't turn left). This first section is attractive, with views of Penkiln Burn and mixed woodland. The road up the Glen is very pretty. It is also a dead-end so remember to take a right turn after two miles (there is only one right turn). When you meet the A712, turn left. The route is a well-graded climb to Clatteringshaws Loch. On the way, you pass the Wild Goat Park where wild goats congregate during the tourist season hoping to be fed.

The visitor centre at Clatteringshaws Loch has excellent wildlife displays, outside picnic tables and a tearoom. The loch itself was formed in 1935 when the River Dee was dammed. The water is piped to Glenlee power station. After Clatteringshaws Loch Visitor Centre, continue up the A712 for just over a mile then turn left up a minor road signed 'Glenlee'. After Glenlee, it's only two miles to St John's Town of Dalry.

Turn right at the T junction in the village then left at the A762. When you get to the power station, turn right to cross the river (Water of Ken), joining the A713 to get to St John's Town of Dalry. Dalry is a quiet village with a good pub doing bar food, a hotel, shops and a number of tearooms in summer.

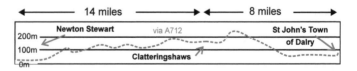

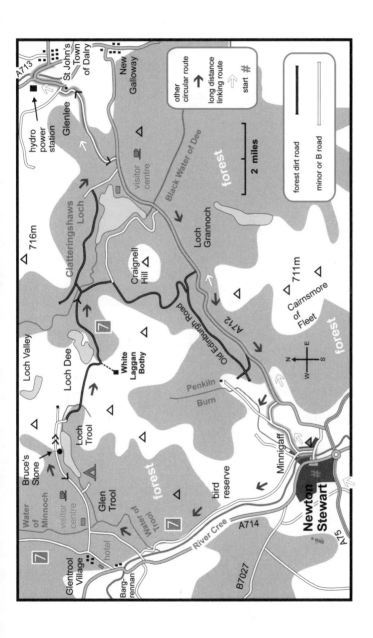

DALRY TO DRUMLANRIG CASTLE

Northern option – Dalry to Drumlanrig Castle via Lorg
Route grading: **Varied – mountain bike** (31 miles, red
arrows)
(Dalry is also known as St John's Town of Dalry)
(Route circular with page 24)

Leave Dalry, going east on the A702, but turn left on to the
B7000. Refer to the map, paying attention to the detailed
notes. The route via Lorg requires you to walk, pushing your
bike for just over a mile. Skilled young people with expensive
mountain bikes might be able to cycle. It is worth it, though,
because it gives access to a lovely little remote road, where
meeting a car would be most unusual. Warm and waterproof
clothing, a bit of food and the ability to fix punctures would be
a good idea.

After the junction with the triangular patch of grass (see
map), there are several ways to get to Drumlanrig. Use the
notes on the map to locate the junctions.

Drumlanrig Castle is a fine building of pink sandstone,
standing in the woods of Nithsdale. It was completed in 1691
and the owner's (William Douglas's) son, James Douglas, performed a crucial role in the Treaty of Union between England
and Scotland. The formal gardens are lovely, and the castle has
many beautiful rooms containing, amongst other things,
Rembrant's masterpiece: *An Old Woman Reading*. There is also a
tearoom in the former kitchen.

DALRY TO DRUMLANRIG CASTLE

Central option – Dalry to Drumlanrig Castle via Moniaive
Route grading: **Hilly** (27 miles, black arrows)
(Dalry is also known as St John's Town of Dalry)

Leave town on the A702. Continue on this road for just over
two miles and turn left for Lochinvar. After you pass the loch
and a small historic schoolhouse, turn right at every public
road junction until you get to Moniaive.

Moniaive has two hotels serving food and a Post
Office/shop. Keep straight on in Moniaive, passing in front of
the Craigdarroch Arms Hotel, signed 'Thornhill'; take the left

turn immediately after this, signed 'Tynron'. In Tynron, make sure you cross over the river (Shinnel Water).

You will now join the busy A702 for a further mile, before turning left at Penpont for Drumlanrig Castle. If you are not going to the castle but heading for Mennock, the Scar Water road is really beautiful but quite hilly.

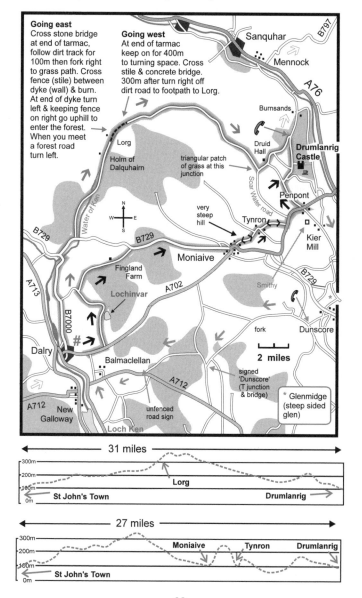

Going east
Cross stone bridge at end of tarmac, follow dirt track for 100m then fork right to grass path. Cross fence (stile) between dyke (wall) & burn. At end of dyke turn left & keeping fence on right go uphill to enter the forest. When you meet a forest road turn left.

Going west
At end of tarmac keep on for 400m to turning space. Cross stile & concrete bridge. 300m after turn right off dirt road to footpath to Lorg.

Sanquhar

Mennock

Burnsands

Druid Hall

Drumlanrig Castle

Lorg

Holm of Dalquhairn

triangular patch of grass at this junction

Scar Water road

Penpont

Water of Ken

very steep hill

Tynron

Kier Mill

B729

B729

Moniaive

Fingland Farm

A702

Smithy

B729

A713

Lochinvar

B7000

fork

Dunscore

Dalry

#

Balmaclellan

2 miles

A712

A712

signed 'Dunscore' (T junction & bridge)

* Glenmidge (steep sided glen)

New Galloway

unfenced road sign

Loch Ken

31 miles

300m
200m
100m
0m

Lorg

St John's Town

Drumlanrig

27 miles

300m
200m
100m
0m

Moniaive   Tynron   Drumlanrig

St John's Town

DRUMLANRIG CASTLE TO DALRY

Southern option – Drumlanrig Castle to Dalry via Dunscore
Route grading: **Varied** (34 miles)
(Dalry is also known as St John's Town of Dalry)
(Route circular with page 22)

Leave Drumlanrig via the west back entry, passing a woodland walks sign and a pond. Turn left on to the public road. After this, keep on to Penpont. Cross the A702 and continue to Keir Mill. Look out for a brass plaque on the smithy where Kirkpatrick MacMillan (the inventor of the bicycle) worked, just before reaching Keir Mill. You might also like to look for MacMillan's gravestone in Keir Mill (instructions on next page).

After Keir Mill, the route continues south, following the River Nith until you turn right at Glenmidge. Midges may not be present, but the glen is easily identifiable as the hills by the road suddenly get very steep. After this, cross the B729 to Dunscore (village shop, real ale in the George Hotel).

The correct route going west out of Dunscore is a descent to Cairn Water. A climb south (church and graveyard) is the wrong way. West of Dunscore, the route is a narrow quiet road through moorland and forest until you reach the A712. At Balmaclellan, there's a shop. The tearooms of St John's Town of Dalry are not far either.

Drumlanrig Castle is a fine mansion of pink sandstone, standing in the woods of Nithsdale. It was completed in 1691 under the orders of William Douglas. He died in 1695, ruined it was said by the expense of building it. His son, James Douglas, performed a crucial role in the Treaty of Union between England and Scotland, and some of the negotiations took place at the castle. Cyclists from Edinburgh may notice that the layout of the castle is the same as George Heriot's school in Edinburgh, which was designed by the architect William Wallace (who died in 1631).

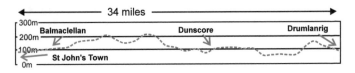

DRUMLANRIG CASTLE TO DALRY

The formal gardens are lovely. There is a walk to a lake. The castle eventually passed to the Dukes of Buccleuch and it is due to them that the castle has become a treasure house full of works of art, containing, amongst other things, Rembrant's masterpiece: *An Old Woman Reading*. A Da Vinci painting, *Madonna with the Yardwinder*, was stolen from Drumlanrig in 2003 and has not yet been recovered.

The village of Keir Mill was where the world's first pedal-powered bicycle was invented. Prior to this, there had only been hobby horses – you pushed on the ground with your feet. 160 years ago, Kirkpatrick MacMillan invented pedals. You might like to look for his gravestone, which is in the old graveyard. This is down a lane on the right, 50 metres after the church (by a 30 mph sign). It's the only grey gravestone. A copy of his bicycle is in the cycle museum in Drumlanrig Castle, together with many other bicycles, all of later date.

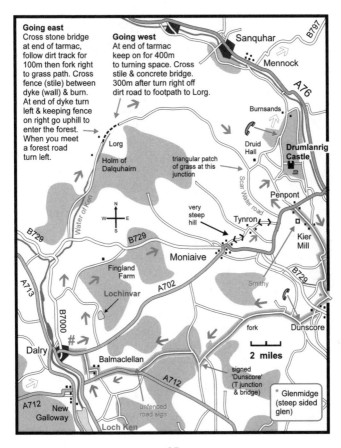

Going east
Cross stone bridge at end of tarmac, follow dirt track for 100m then fork right to grass path. Cross fence (stile) between dyke (wall) & burn. At end of dyke turn left & keeping fence on right go uphill to enter the forest. When you meet a forest road turn left.

Going west
At end of tarmac keep on for 400m to turning space. Cross stile & concrete bridge. 300m after turn right off dirt road to footpath to Lorg.

Sanquhar
Mennock
Burnsands
Druid Hall
Drumlanrig Castle
Lorg
Holm of Dalquhairn
triangular patch of grass at this junction
Scar Water road
Penpont
very steep hill
Tynron
Kier Mill
Water of Ken
B729
B729
Moniaive
Fingland Farm
Lochinvar
A702
Smithy
B729
A713
B7000
fork
Dunscore
Dalry
Balmaclellan
2 miles
A712
signed 'Dunscore' (T junction & bridge)
* Glenmidge (steep sided glen)
A712 New Galloway
unfenced road sign
Loch Ken

25

LOCHINVAR CIRCULAR

A circular route of 12 miles, very attractive views
Route grading: **Hilly** (12 miles)

This is a lovely little route of 12 miles. If anything could convince you that cycling in Dumfries and Galloway is just wonderful, this route certainly should. It includes two miles on the A702. This need not concern you too much, as the A702 is a relatively quiet road.

There are fine views over the Water of Ken and its associated lochs. These lochs were created shortly before the Second World War, in the first large-scale hydroelectric scheme in Scotland.

Leave town going east on the A702 but turn left on to the B7000 before you leave the village. There are a few ups and downs but the tendency is generally up. As you get higher, the Water of Ken comes into view, with the hills of the Rhinns of Kells behind.

There is still some climbing after the second road junction (a right turn). The route crosses moorland. The Southern Upland Way walking route crosses the cycle route at the next junction (turn right again).

After this, the tiny single track road winds across the moor to Lochinvar, passing a small historic schoolhouse. When you descend to the A702, turn right again for the final two miles to Dalry (also known as St John's Town of Dalry).

St John's Town of Dalry is really a village. It is named after St John's church of the Knights Templar, which stood in the area. The village changed in the late eighteenth century, when building was sponsored by the Earl of Galloway. Among the remains of the old church is the Gordon Aisle for Sir James Gordon of Lochinvar.

St John's Town of Dalry is part of the Galloway hydroelectric scheme, which was built shortly before the Second World War, and includes the Earlstoun Power Station (see map).

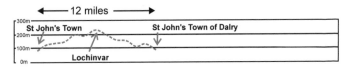

LOCHINVAR CIRCULAR

There are plenty of places to stay in Dalry, including The Clachan Inn and the Lochinvar Hotel, plus a number of B&Bs. There are also several tearooms and shops.

> Oh, young Lochinvar is come out of the west;
> Through all the wide border his steed was the best;
> And, save his good broadsword, he weapon had none;
> He rode all unarmed, and he rode all alone.
> So faithful in love, and so dauntless in war,
> There never was knight like the young Lochinvar!
>
> Sir Walter Scott, 'Lochinvar'
> (from *Marmion*, Canto V)

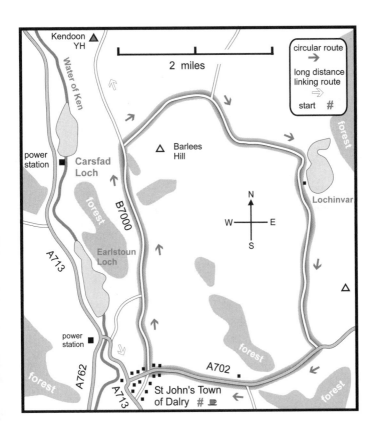

FOREST OF AE

Forest and river views, quiet roads, pubs and tearooms
Route grading: **Varied** (30 miles)

The description here assumes starting at the village of Ae. Tearooms in Thornhill or at Drumlanrig Castle would make a good choice for lunch. We also had a beer in the afternoon at the pub in Auldgirth.

Leave Ae with the pub on your right. After the 30 mph sign, turn left then keep straight on, signed 'Loch Ettrick'. There is a steady climb, with a mixture of forest and open views. After the left turn at Loch Ettrick, there's a descent with great views. Following this, there's a number of ways you could go wrong. Head for the castle and the church if you make a mistake in the next section.

Bear left at a sign for 'Closeburn 5', then bear right at a sign for 'Closeburn 1¼'. There's a view of Closeburn Castle on the right. Ignore the left turn to Park but turn right at a newish house with a paddock. Pass a church with a tower on the right. At the next junction, go left, then right around the school. After half a mile, turn left to cross the railway opposite a rusty field gate. Take care crossing the A76, then turn right at Kirkland Farm to continue north to Thornhill.

Thornhill is an attractive town, with a choice of pubs and tearooms. Alternatively, you could continue north to Drumlanrig Castle (description page 24).

To continue, cross the River Nith on the A702 going west, then immediately turn left to a minor road for Keir Mill. You might like to visit Kirkpatrick MacMillan's grave in the old graveyard at Keir Mill (inventor of the bicycle, see page 24). This is down a lane by a 30 mph sign on the opposite side from the church.

Turn left in Keir Mill to continue south. The hills are gentle but they get steeper near Glenmidge. Bear left at all the junctions. There's a descent to Auldgirth, where you cross the River Nith. The pub here has a beer garden.

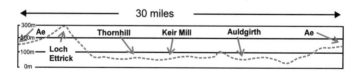

FOREST OF AE

From Auldgirth, it's a climb to Dalswinton then a descent with good views. Turn left near a Victorian school building at the sign for 'Amisfield 3'. Bear right after a bridge, then turn left at a tower (former windmill), then left again after Auchencairn for Ae.

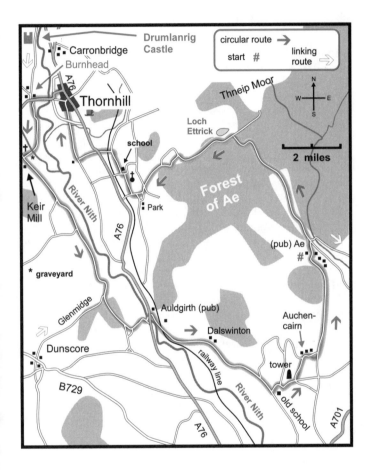

AE TO TUSHIELAW

Described as a linking section but a lovely remote route
– very quiet
Route grading: **Hilly** (39 miles)

The linking section only is described here but there is also a circular route (see map). The A708 is not usually busy. There is a possible short cut using a forest road by the Tibbie Shiels Inn (top of map).

Between Ae and Boreland, it's a maze of minor roads. These instructions are intended to get you through fairly simply, avoiding the A701. Leave Ae, taking the road on the north side of the Water of Ae. To get to this, head for the wooden Forestry Commission buildings just north of the village. At the A701, turn right then immediately left, taking a minor road by the side of the Ae Inn (bar food, open all day).

Past the houses, the road turns into a stony track. Go along this, then use a footpath by a gate. You come to a concrete entry road (Barony College), then meet a public road again. Turn right here. Following this, keep straight on at the other road junctions, following signs for Templand.

In Templand, cross straight over the B7020. At Millhousebridge, bear left to cross the river then straight on, following a sign: Lockerbie. 300 metres after this, turn right. Turn left at the next junction to pass over the motorway. There's another right turn to get you to the B723. After this, the navigation is easy but the cycling gets more difficult.

The tiny scattered settlement of Eskdalemuir lies on the route of one of the Roman roads which headed north towards the Forth–Clyde Valley. Since the days of the Roman Empire, it's been off the beaten track.

Eskdalemuir's surprise is the Samye Ling Tibetan Centre, founded in 1967. This is the largest Buddhist monastery in the Western world. At the heart of it is a spectacular temple built in the 1980s. There's a tearoom and visitors are welcome to look around.

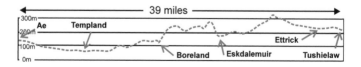

North again is Eskdalemuir Observatory, which opened in 1908. It monitors the UK's geomagnetic field. It moved here from Kew Observatory because the power supply to London electric trams upset the readings. Nowadays the observatory also measures solar radiation and atmospheric pollution.

North of the observatory is a stretch of lonely road until you get to the village of Ettrick. There are no facilities, but a few miles north the Tushielaw Inn does real ale and bar meals. This is unlikely to be open on winter weekdays. If that is closed, there is also a pub and shop further along the B7009 at Ettrick Bridge (map next page) and of course lots of facilities beyond this in Selkirk.

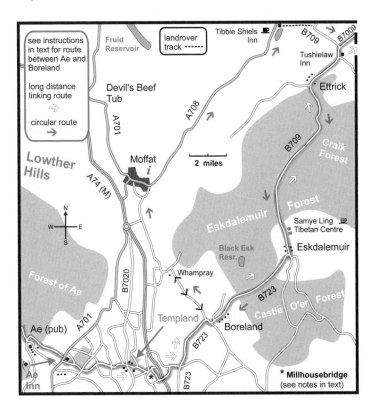

SELKIRK, TUSHIELAW AND ASHKIRK

A beautiful quiet route by Ettrick Water, returning over
the hills via Ashkirk
Route grading: **Hilly** (39 miles)

The Ettrick and Yarrow Waters are both tributaries of the
River Tweed, joining it north of Selkirk. Sheep farming is an
important rural activity around here and the familiar black and
white border collie is still a working dog.

Begin in Selkirk in the town centre, by the statue of Sir
Walter Scott, and go downhill, signed 'Bowhill 3' and
'Peebles/Moffat'. Turn left near the bottom of the hill to the
B7009, signed 'Ettrick Bridge'. Ettrick Bridge is the home of
the former Liberal leader and the first speaker of the Scottish
Parliament, Sir David Steel.

Ettrick Bridge was also the birthplace of the author, James
Hogg. Perhaps not so well known as his friend, Sir Walter
Scott, Hogg's best-known work is *Confessions of a Justified
Sinner*. There is a monument nearby and his grave is in the
churchyard. There is a pub and a food shop in Ettrick Bridge.

The Tushielaw Inn is well worth stopping at, as they do bar
lunches, although it probably won't be open during winter
weekdays. Eating would be a good idea, as the hills are getting
near. As you start to get higher, there are fine views of the
rolling border hills. Shortly after Alemoor Loch, turn left
again, signed 'Ashkirk'.

After the climb, you descend to Ashkirk, crossing the river
Ale Water. Turn left before you reach the A7 main road, signed
'Ettrickbridge'. Begin another climb over Woll Rigg, signed
'Ettrickbridge'. After this, it's a right turn with lots of descent to
reach the B7009 leading back to Selkirk. Selkirk has a choice of
pubs and tearooms, though the latter seem to disappear out of
season. The pubs, however, always seem to be able to produce
cups of tea and coffee if requested.

In Selkirk you can visit Clapperton Daylight Photographic
Studio (historic photographs) and Halliwell's House Museum

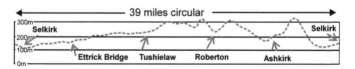

(eighteenth-century houses), or Sir Walter Scott's Courtroom. Selkirk has the Common Riding in June, when horse riders ride the Marches and re-enact the story of Flodden.

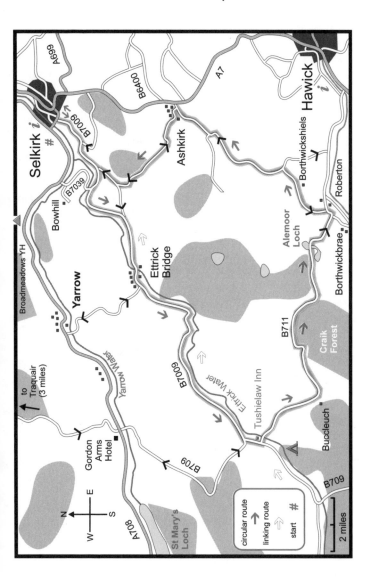

SELKIRK, DRYBURGH AND MELROSE

A scenic circular with historic places to visit
Route grading: **Hilly** (23 miles)

This route takes you east from Selkirk, calling at Melrose. At Eildon, it meets National Cycle Network Route 1, where you have the option of visiting Dryburgh Abbey.

In Selkirk town square, pass in front of the County Hotel, following the sign for Hawick. Immediately after the hotel, turn left towards a church. Pass the church and a police station then turn right up Shawpark Road at another church. Climb steeply for a mile to a radio mast, then turn right at a T junction (half-crown corner). When you meet the A699, turn right then left, signed 'Midlem'. After this, the route is straightforward until you get to Eildon.

If you are going to Dryburgh Abbey, turn right in Eildon and follow National Cycle Network Route 1 through Newtown St Boswells. Follow NCN (1) signs crossing the A68 and the River Tweed. If you are continuing on the circle to Melrose, turn left in Eildon. A little way up the hill you will meet a gated road (NCN).

Cross the A6091 into Melrose, following cycle signs and passing the youth hostel into the town square. Continue on, following NCN signs to Darnick. In Darnick, leave the National Cycle Network and go up Broomilees Road. This takes you over the A6091 bypass road and up the hill past Kaeside Farm.

After Kaeside Farm, take the left fork, turn right at the next junction towards Fallonside. You meet a gate on the road. Go through this. Turn right down a dirt track under an electricity line. Pass a small loch. Descend to the A7. Cycle on the A7 cyclepath to Selkirk. Just after Selkirk Glass, turn left to Raeburn Place and follow the road through the housing estate back to the start.

Dryburgh Abbey is in a lovely setting in a bend in the River Tweed. It was founded in 1150. Both it and Melrose Abbey are beautiful ruins. Abbotsford (see map) is Sir Walter Scott's house. It is open in summer only.

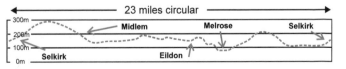

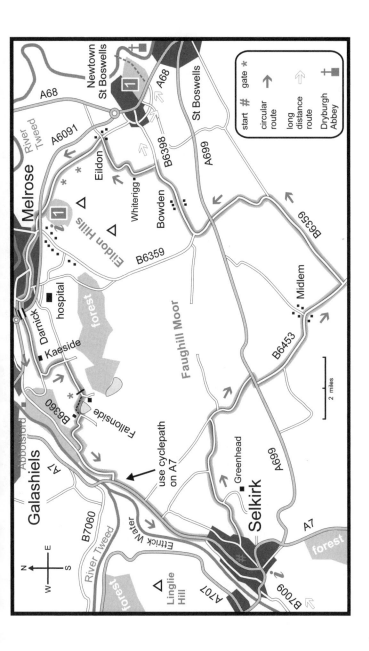

FOUR ABBEYS CYCLE ROUTE

Or an easier three abbeys cycle route
Route grading: **Hilly** (55 or 41 miles)

There are two ways to get between Melrose and Dryburgh Abbey. For a short ride of 10 miles, you could go out on one and return on the other. This route should be signposted.

Scott's View Route – leave Melrose, going east (downstream) between the river and the abbey. After that, follow Tweed Cycleway signs, keeping near to the river and crossing it on the old bridge near a railway viaduct.

Newtown St Boswells Route – leave Melrose town square by the West Port, going south-east past the youth hostel and cross the bypass road. Follow National Cycle Network signs. Dryburgh Abbey was founded 1150 and is in a scenic setting in a bend in the River Tweed.

Between Dryburgh Abbey and Kelso it's rolling country, passing Smailholm Tower (sixteenth century), which contains tapestries and Walter Scott figures. Before Kelso is Floors Castle, designed by William Adam. It has an excellent restaurant. Leave Kelso, crossing the River Tweed, and turn right on to the A699 for a little way. You will pass the abbey just before the river.

Two miles before Nisbet is a decision point: are you going to Jedburgh? If so, there are some hills in front of you after you cross the Kalemouth suspension bridge. Cross the river, turn right on to the A698, then immediately left off it to the B6401. Turn right just before Morebattle. Cessford Castle, which is another ruin, marks the start of a long climb, after which you are only a mile from Jedburgh.

Jedburgh Abbey is the finest surviving medieval building in Scotland. Castle Jail and Mary Queen of Scots House are also worth a visit. To leave, go north on the A68 but turn right off it. There is a pub at Ancrum, but after that nothing until Melrose. Mainly it's uphill, until the Eildon Hills for the final descent.

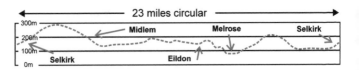

36

FOUR ABBEYS CYCLE ROUTE

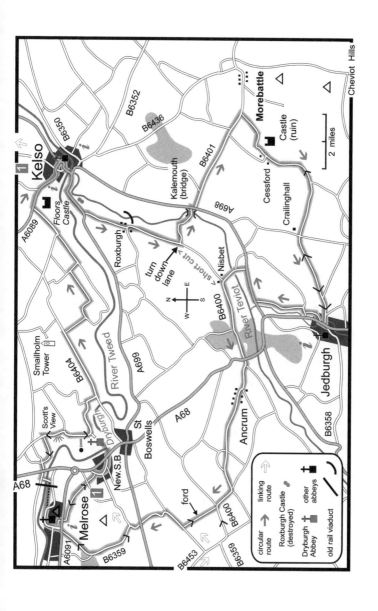

KELSO TO DUNS

Easy rolling terrain, woods and farms
Route grading: **Easy** (17 miles)

The map opposite also shows a cycle route to Berwick-upon-Tweed (32 miles). This is signed as 'National Cycle Network Route 1' and is not described in the text.

Kelso has a particularly elegant town square. The bridge over the River Tweed was the prototype of London's Waterloo Bridge, being designed by the same engineer, John Rennie. Kelso Abbey was built around 1128, and was one of the finest examples of Romanesque architecture. It was finally finished and dedicated in 1243. One of the largest and richest abbeys in Scotland, it had an important library in medieval times. Near Kelso is Floors Castle, designed by William Adam. It has an excellent restaurant, which can be accessed without paying the admission charge for the Castle.

From Kelso, the route to Duns follows the National Cycle Network as far as Eccles, then it turns north to a minor road beside a haulage depot. (The route to Berwick turns south.) The route between Eccles and Duns is straightforward, but some of the road junctions have no signs so it is necessary to count the turnings (see map).

The A697 crossing is not straight over but right and left – take care. Look out for a stork on a building at Sinclair's Hill (turn left). After this, you pass Mungo's Walls and Wedderburn Castle, before rolling into Duns.

Duns has B&Bs, tearooms and hotels. Manderston House is near, which features the only silver staircase in the world and large, beautifully kept gardens. It has a tearoom, of course. Going to Dunbar you can avoid the A6112 by going through Duns Castle nature reserve. Remain in the public areas, and turn right after the lake.

Travelling south, entry to Duns Castle nature reserve from the B6365 is signed 'car park for reserve'. The sign is by the base of a stone pillar. After a kilometre, turn left to go south of the lake.

38

KELSO TO DUNS

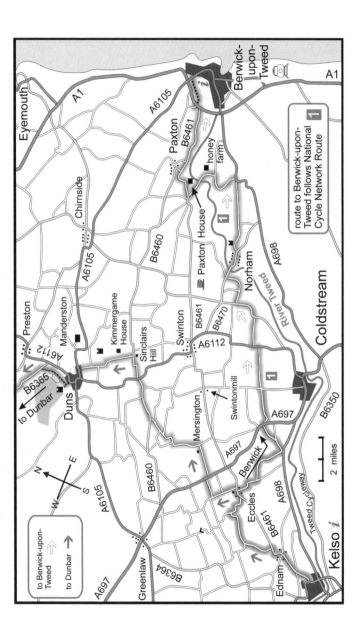

39

DUNBAR TO ABBEY ST BATHANS

Quiet – but fierce hills and surprising scenery
Route grading: **Hilly** – any bike (34 miles)

Dunbar is a railway station on the Edinburgh-to-London line but not all trains stop there. The eastern end of the Lammermuir Hills reaches the sea here and the escarpments plunge from 300 metres to nearly sea level.

Starting at Dunbar, avoid cycling along the A1. The minor road to Spott leaves Dunbar from the High Street east of the train station, by a red sandstone church. If you are driving, start at Spott. From Spott, the road descends The Brunt, then climbs up the other side. Turn right for Elmscleugh Farm – the various dogs, geese, hens, etc. will make a noise as you pass. There's a climb of 174 metres after this.

You enter a forest. You can go either way but the right fork takes you near Cranshaws tearoom. At Ellemford Bridge, you can go down a forest dirt road by the river, or continue two miles on the B6355 to reach Abbey St Bathans on a hilly minor road.

Abbey St Bathans is the site of a twelfth-century Cistercian priory. The village is surrounded by ancient oak woods. There is a restaurant, a picnic area and a trout farm.

Leave Abbey St Bathans on the road east (upstream). You pass an off-road driving school then turn left for Oldhamstocks. In Oldhamstocks, turn right for Innerwick then follow signs for Innerwick. The building in the distance by the sea is Torness nuclear power station. Keep straight on through Innerwick.

Beyond the village, look for a piece of poetry by the left-hand side of the road. At the next T junction, turn left, signed 'Elmscleugh', then right, signed 'The Brunt'. Keep straight on to Spott.

Dunbar was the birthplace of John Muir, founder of the national parks system in the USA. You can visit his house in Dunbar. There's also a modern swimming pool and a choice of

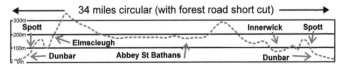

tearooms and pubs. You might like to look at the harbour too.

Coming from Duns, you can miss out the A6112 (see page 38) by going through the grounds of Duns Castle. This is a nature reserve. Remain in the public areas of the castle grounds and turn right after the lake.

Going south to Duns, entry to the castle and the nature reserve from the B6365 is signed 'car park for reserve'. The sign is beside the broken base of a stone pillar. After a kilometre, turn left to go south of the lake.

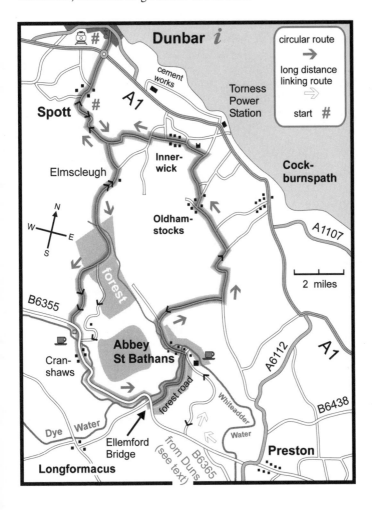

ROUTES FROM EDINBURGH

DISTANCES AND ROUTE GRADING

CHAPTER 2

ROUTES FROM EDINBURGH

This chapter describes routes in Fife and the Lothians. The Union Canal towpath route, which connects Edinburgh and Glasgow, is described as far as Falkirk. For the canal towpath route between Falkirk and Glasgow, see the Glasgow chapter (page 65).

Edinburgh suffers from heavy road traffic, but despite this there are a number of quiet ways to go on a bike. These make use of canal towpaths and converted railway lines. The routes run through quiet strips of green in the city, taking you to minor roads in the Lothians, where traffic is quite light. The scenery is as attractive as any in Scotland. The routes pass reservoirs in the Pentland and Moorfoot hills, woodlands and beautiful beaches.

There is a wide choice of cycle routes in Fife. Some around Dunfermline and Kirkcaldy are more urban in character, but the east Fife routes are rural, with sea views. Catch a train to Leuchars, just north of St Andrews.

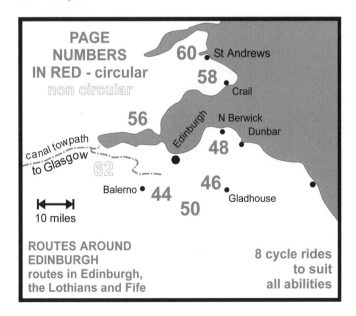

PAGE NUMBERS IN RED - circular
non circular

60 St Andrews
58
Crail
56
N Berwick
Edinburgh
Dunbar
48
canal towpath to Glasgow
62
Balerno 44
46
Gladhouse
50

10 miles

ROUTES AROUND EDINBURGH
routes in Edinburgh, the Lothians and Fife

8 cycle rides to suit all abilities

PENTLAND HILLS RESERVOIRS

An easy off-road bike route with great scenery
Route grading: **Varied – mountain bike** (20 miles)

This first section to Balerno is signed 'National Cycle
Network Route 75'. At Tollcross, in central Edinburgh, start
from the King's Theatre. Go up Gilmore Place opposite. Take
the first right by a church to Lower Gilmore Place, then join
the Union Canal towpath. After two miles, the canal goes over
a high aqueduct (walk). Soon after, leave the canal by crossing
a footbridge over it.

Now you are on an old railway line by the Water of Leith.
The route crosses access roads a couple of times. When this
happens, continue in the same direction, looking for the dirt
path on the other side. This section ends in Balerno.

Turn left on to Bridge Road (the Cycle Network goes
right), then turn left up Bavelaw Road, signed 'Malleny House
Garden'. Keep straight on up the hill to leave Balerno. At Red
Moss Wildlife Reserve, take the left fork towards the hills.
After 400 metres, turn left at Threipmuir car park and go
down a rough track. Continue along by the shore of
Threipmuir Reservoir to the overflow sluiceway. Use the little
iron bridge to cross the sluiceway, then bear left to Harlaw
Reservoir. Cross the dam.

Leave Harlaw Reservoir by bearing left, past a red
sandstone cottage. After 300 metres, bear left to the public
road. When you see the sign 'Public Path to Glencorse', go in
the opposite direction. Turn right at the next junction, by
electricity pylons. After this, bear right at a white house, just
before a steep descent to Currie.

After 500 metres, you cross a burn on a stone bridge, then find
yourself in a farmyard. Turn sharp right to a rough track, then
turn east again to Cubbiedean Reservoir. After this, you descend
steeply to Torduff Reservoir – go round the west side.

After Torduff, there is a steep descent to Torduff Road.
Turn left to cross over the city bypass. After this, keep straight

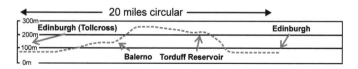

on down Bonaly Road, passing modern houses, and turn right at the T junction at the foot on to Woodhall Road (opposite West Colinton House). After 300 metres, turn left down a footpath. This is opposite a white house with black timbers. Walk down the steps, then turn left down some more steps just before the bridge carrying the public road. When you are on the same level as the Water of Leith, cross the river on a footbridge.

Follow the same route you came out on to get back to Tollcross after this. Keep to the main railway path as far as the Union Canal, then turn right (east). Because of the layout of the bridge footpath, this right turn when you meet the canal is actually a double left turn.

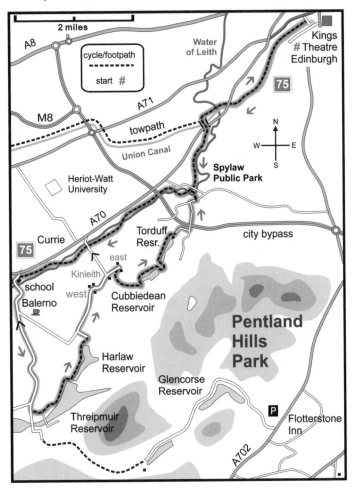

WEST LINTON AND TEMPLE

A scenic route using quiet roads in Midlothian
Route grading: **Varied – any bike** (39 miles)

Set between the Moorfoot and Pentland Hills, the countryside
south of Edinburgh is attractive. This route is surprisingly
rural. There are a few short sections on main roads but most
of the route is on minor roads, with some of it on a converted
railway line. The start of the route is near the junction of the
A6094 and the B7003 (Roslin Glen road). Go along the B7003
from Rosewell and you will see the cyclepath sign.

Start off by following the sign, travelling south-west
towards Penicuik. After a while, the cyclepath takes you
through a tunnel by the paper mill at Auchendinny. It runs on
to Penicuik, ending at a housing estate. Keep on the flat
cyclepath until you have passed a pond then turn left to go
through a small housing development.

At the main road, turn left, signed 'Peebles'. (Turn right to
get to Penicuik. Penicuik has a choice of shops and a number
of places you can get food. There is also a bike shop.) Turn
right off the A701 at the top of the hill, signed 'West Linton'.
This quiet road crosses Auchencorth Moss, giving views of the
Pentland Hills. Go straight on at the next junction to West
Linton. This attractive village has a tearoom, and two hotels
which do bar lunches.

Leave West Linton the way you entered, on Deanfoot
Road. At the first crossroads, by Deepsyke Forest, turn right,
signed 'Lamanca'. At the A701, turn left, then after two miles
turn right, signed 'Eddleston via Shiplaw'. This next section is
quite hilly but very scenic. When you get to the A703, turn
left, but after 1.5 miles turn right off it, signed 'Temple and
Gorebridge'.

Ignore a right turn for Moorfoot (farm) but turn right after
this, signed 'Gladhouse'. Pass the reservoir, which is visible
through trees. At a T junction, turn left, signed 'Temple and
Gorebridge'. After Temple, turn left over a bridge, then right,

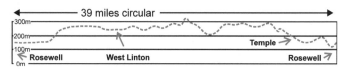

signed 'Carrington'. In Carrington, turn left by a church, then after a mile turn left again at crossroads. Follow the public road round and cross the A6094.

Continue along this minor road then turn right at a staggered junction. Shortly after this, you will cycle over the Penicuik cyclepath on a stone bridge. You can either rejoin the cyclepath at the bridge (dismount) or continue descending to Roslin Glen, turning right on to the B7003 to get back to Rosewell.

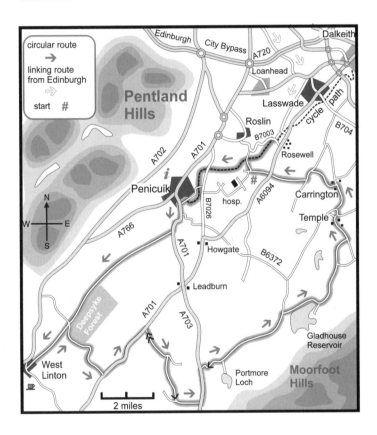

BEACHES AND CASTLES

An East Lothian circular on minor roads
Route grading: **Easy** (33 miles)

You can get a train to Longniddry from Edinburgh. East Lothian has beautiful beaches and many interesting places to visit, including castles, a restored watermill and the Museum of Flight. The main roads are busy. The railway can be useful to shorten distances.

Leave Longniddry on the B6363. From the train station, turn left then go west along the A198 for 400 metres, turning left again underneath the railway. There's an easy climb for 500 metres then you turn left again to a minor road (no sign). After two miles, turn right at a T junction then take the left fork in the road up a hill. Turn left at the top. At a T junction, turn left on to the A6137, then take the first right to the B1343.

On the right is the Hopetoun Monument – which is worth the climb. Continue to Athelstaneford. Turn right and then left at a staggered junction. Turn left in Athelstaneford (Heritage Centre) after the school. Leave Athelstaneford on the B1343 for a mile then turn right to the B1377 towards East Linton. The Museum of Flight is nearby (Vulcan bomber, airship, Concorde, tearoom). East Linton is an attractive village, with hotels and shops.

Leave East Linton on the B1407, following signs for Preston Mill. Have a look at the restored watermill. 300 metres after this, turn left on to a minor road, leaving the B1407. After two miles turn left at the top of the hill then immediately turn right. After this, take the first left then the first right to continue straight on towards the hill of North Berwick Law. (There are plenty of facilities in North Berwick.)

Leave North Berwick by the High School, which is on the B1347. Follow signs for North Berwick Law, the obvious conical hill. Turn right to a minor road which passes down the side of the school. After a couple of miles, turn right again at Kingston to pass over the railway line. Just before the railway

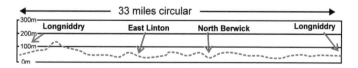

line crossing there is another possible diversion to visit Dirleton Castle. There's also a very attractive beach at Yellowcraigs in the country park, just north of the Dirleton village (see map).

After crossing the railway, you are briefly on the B1345, turning left then right off it near Fenton Barns turkey farm. The B1345 is not quiet. After this, you turn left at the next three junctions. Around here you are quite near Drem Railway Station so you could go back from there or continue along to Longniddry on the B1377 to complete the circle.

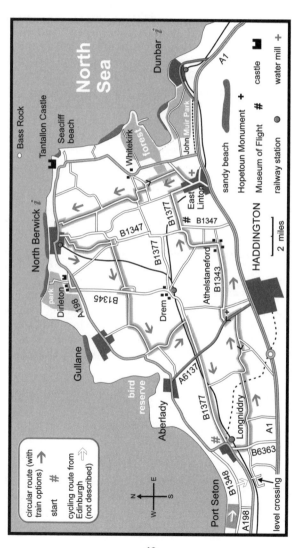

ROUND EDINBURGH OFF-ROAD

Explore a canal towpath, four old railway lines and the Pentland Hills, some urban sections but great scenery too! Route grading: **Varied – mountain bike** *(37 miles)*

This route uses the National Cycle Network, Route 75, from Edinburgh to Balerno. After this, it crosses the Pentland Hills. The return to Edinburgh is on the Penicuik to Dalkeith Cycle Route, then via National Cycle Network, Route 1, to central Edinburgh. Much of the route is really beautiful, for example cycling through woodland by the Water of Leith, or crossing the Pentland Hills. There are urban sections too, but most of the route is a park of some kind. Finding your way is quite easy until the Flotterstone Inn, after which more care is needed. The Cycle Network sections should be signed, but pay attention to the maps and instructions, as some signs could be missing. Doing the route anticlockwise is best.

TOLLCROSS – BALERNO (8 MILES, NATIONAL ROUTE 75)

Start from the King's Theatre at Tollcross in central Edinburgh. Go up Gilmore Place opposite. Take the first right by a church to Lower Gilmore Place and join the Union Canal towpath. After two miles, you go over a high aqueduct (walk). Soon after this, cross a footbridge over the canal and the Lanark Road (A70). Keep right along a disused railway line by the Water of Leith, passing through a tunnel. The route crosses access roads a couple of times. When this happens, continue in the same direction, looking for the dirt path on the other side. This section ends by Balerno High School in Bridge Road, where you leave Route 75.

BALERNO – AUCHENDINNY (10 MILES, NOT SIGNED)

At Balerno High School, turn left on to Bridge Road. After 400 metres, turn left up Bavelaw Road, signed 'Malleny House

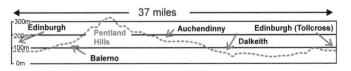

Garden'. Keep straight on up the hill to leave Balerno. At Red Moss Wildlife Reserve, take the left fork towards the hills. Cross Threipmuir Reservoir, then at the T junction at the top of Beech Avenue turn left, and then right (right-of-way sign). Follow the made-up path across the hills. After a mile, it becomes a rough track, but it is still rideable. At Loganlea Reservoir, the route becomes a road again. Follow this to the Flotterstone Inn on the A702, then turn right. After a little way, turn left off the A702 to an unmarked dirt lane by a cottage – do not cycle up the hill. Bear right at the first junction then turn right at the farm. When you meet a minor

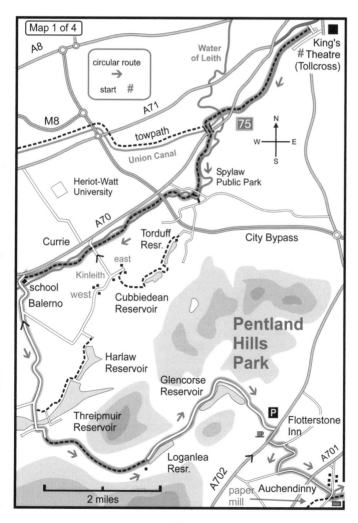

road, turn left then cross the A701 to Auchendinny. In Auchendinny, go straight over and down to the paper mill – the cycle route runs past it. Turn left on to the cycle route, cycling past the paper mill.

AUCHENDINNY – DALKEITH (7 MILES)
There is a fenced section at the paper mill, then a tunnel. The path is broken by a road junction at Rosewell – cross over and you will see it again. After this, it passes under the A6094. Although it seems to end at Bonnyrigg, keep straight on in the same direction. Cross Campview Road and go down by a swing park and a station platform with flower beds. Cross Dundas Street and go down Waverley Court. Soon it becomes obvious that you are on a cyclepath again.

You pass over a bypass road and end in a yard. Turn right down a dirt track then left to another cyclepath. Now you are cycling on National Cycle Network Route 1.

Keep straight on past a station platform. Turn right at another cyclepath T junction. When you meet the public road, turn left and follow the A6094 and National Cycle Network Route 1 signs to get through Dalkeith.

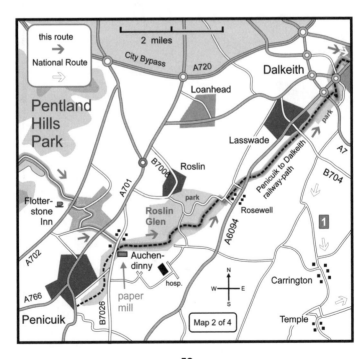

DALKEITH – TOLLCROSS (12 MILES)

(Follow Route 1 bike signs.) In Dalkeith, keep straight on through two sets of traffic lights (signed 'Whitecraig', 'Musselburgh'). Bear right in front of Dalkeith Park, then cross the River South Esk. At a roundabout, take the second exit signed 'Thornybank'. Turn left on to the B6414. Then turn left to the Smeaton cyclepath. This becomes a dirt surface just before it ends at Whitecraig.

At the public road, turn left, following the bike sign for Musselburgh. After a quarter of a mile, turn right down Cowpits Road ('River Esk Walkway 2.5'). At the next bend leave the road ('River Esk Walkway 2'). Go under the bypass, then after 200 metres turn left to cross the River Esk on a metal footbridge. Pass under a railway line to a mini-roundabout. Go straight over into a cul-de-sac (new houses).

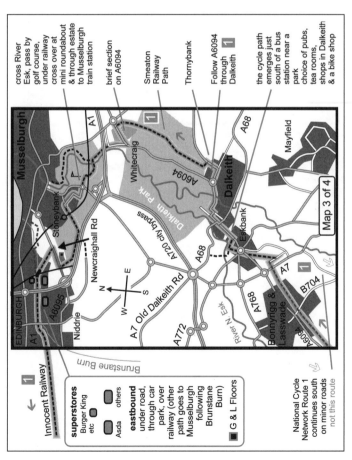

In the cul-de-sac, follow 'Route 1' bike signs to Musselburgh train station keeping gently uphill. At the station, you pass over the railway line to another cyclepath. Follow this for a mile to Newcraighall Road, where you turn right. Shortly after passing GL Floors showroom, turn left through bollards to another cyclepath.

It is planned that this section will be carried over the railway but this has not happened yet. In the meantime, keep under the pylons, leaving the tarmac strip after 300 metres. After 30 metres on the dirt section, turn right through an opening, cross a road, join another cyclepath, cross another road, then cross the railway on a footbridge.

After the footbridge, cross the car park, go through an underpass, then bear right to a dirt-surface cyclepath. Climb gently, cross Duddingston Park South – you are now on the Innocent Cycle Path. Continue along this, crossing Duddingston Road West to central Edinburgh, passing through the Innocent Railway Tunnel. At the end of the tunnel, you can join normal streets or follow the bike route through a housing estate to the Engine Shed Café. After this, follow map directions and Route 1 signs to get to Gilmore Place to complete the circle (see map).

THE PENTLAND HILLS

The Pentlands can seem as remote and beautiful as any of Scotland's hills. They are now a Regional Park. Mountain biking is allowed on marked routes and these are colour-coded as follows: yellow – suitable for cycling; green – subject to erosion, no fierce braking, do not use after prolonged rain; red – risk of collision, cycle under control; blue – you are not allowed to cycle on blue paths.

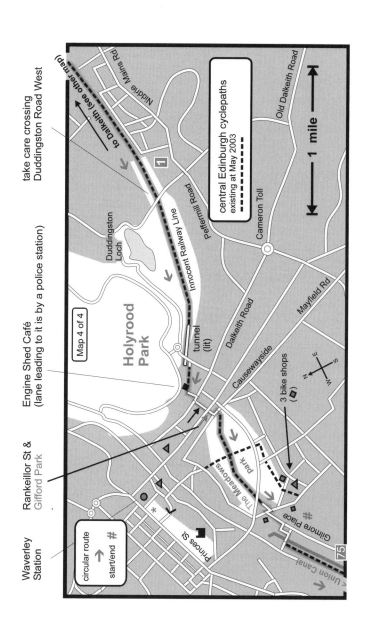

take care crossing
Duddingston Road West

Engine Shed Café
(lane leading to it is by a police station)

Rankeillor St &
Gifford Park

Waverley
Station

to Dalkeith (see other map)

Niddrie Mains Rd

central Edinburgh cyclepaths
existing at May 2003

Old Dalkeith Road

1 mile

Peffermill Road

Innocent Railway Line

Cameron Toll

Duddingston
Loch

Map 4 of 4

Holyrood
Park

tunnel
(lit)

Dalkeith Road

Mayfield Rd

Causewayside

3 bike shops

N
W   E
S

The Meadows

park

Gilmore Place

circular route

start/end

Princes St

Union Canal

75

DUNFERMLINE TO CULROSS

A lovely little route – very little traffic
Route grading: **Varied – any bike** (19 miles)

The first part is on a converted railway line. The route runs from Dunfermline, capital of Scotland in early times, to the preserved seventeenth-century town of Culross. There are views of the Ochil Hills and the Forth Estuary. Pubs can provide bar meals in Culross, where there's also a food shop and attractive places to picnic. The route starts in Dunfermline from a small car park at the beginning of the West Fife Cycleway. This is at William Street.

There is a marked cycle route from Dunfermline train station to William Street via Pittencrieff Public Park. Leave the train station, travelling west through an underpass. At the junction with New Road, keep straight on into Priory Lane, following signs for Andrew Carnegie's birthplace. Go to the left of this then enter the park. Follow the cycle route through the park then continue in the same direction. After four road junctions, turn left at the junction of Ross Lane and Golfdrum Street. Turn right into William Street.

The railway path section needs no directions but you need to be aware of when to leave it. After five miles, you pass over a viaduct near the village of Blairhall. This is the only tarmac surface on the cyclepath. Leave the cyclepath a mile after this, where a bridge with a stone arch crosses over it. Turn left to travel south.

There is a climb with views of the Ochil Hills behind, a gentler section, then a rapid descent to Culross. Take care crossing the A985; go straight across. The final part in Culross is over some picturesque but bumpy stone cobbles. There are many things to see in Culross, including Culross Palace and the Town House.

Leave Culross, travelling east (sea on your right), passing through Low Valleyfield and Torryburn. In Torryburn, pass under a railway bridge; there is a swing park for children by the sea. Turn right here, signed 'Crombie', following a little lane by the sea marked 'cyclists and residents only'. At first, this is a dirt

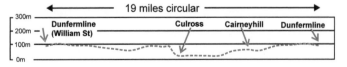

track then it becomes Shoreside Road. Near Crombie Point, the route turns away from the sea, climbing through fields to the A985. At the A985, turn left and use the footpath for a short distance, then shortly before the roundabout turn right to a minor road leading over the railway to Cairniehill. Turn right and cycle through the village then turn left on to Pitdinnie Road. You pass a golf course on the right, and fields on the left. A little over a mile further on, you will meet the railway path again. Turn right onto it to return to Dunfermline.

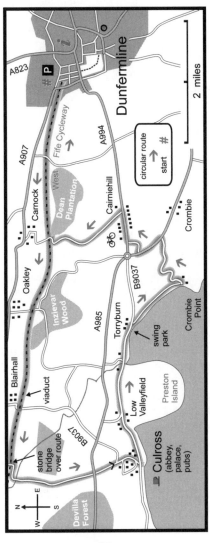

ST ANDREWS, CRAIL AND ANSTRUTHER

Route grading: **Easy – any bike** (37 miles)

Neuk is the old Scots word for corner. The East Neuk fishing villages are set in the natural harbours along the coast. Inland, this is an area of mixed farm and woodland, with sea views.

The route starts with a linking section from St Andrews. The simplest way to get to the start is to follow the A917 south to the edge of the town, at which point the route is signposted.

After three miles, you come to a T junction, where you turn left. At the time of writing there was no sign, but there is no other junction. The next couple of miles to the B9131 are fairly flat. Turn right at this junction. You pass through the tiny hamlet of Dunino. A mile after that, you meet a minor road to the left and are on the circular section.

Fife Cycleways deem this part to be an orange route and you are following these markers from here to Crail. Turn left to the minor road and follow it for three miles. Near here, look out for your right turn onto a dirt track that once was a railway line. Follow this for two miles. The route leaves the rail line after a mile or so and follows farm tracks. It then meets the B9171, where you turn left. Turn left again for a very short distance on to the A917, and then right off it to a tarmac drive leading to Wormiston House. Beyond the house, the surface is bumpier. Turn right onto the public road for Crail. In Crail, follow signs for the harbour.

Crail has plenty going on and lobsters for sale, though these are fairly incompatible with bicycle panniers. The harbour is very pretty. When the time comes to go, you have a short distance on the A917 going northwest, before turning left to the B940 then left to the B9171. This is a blue cycle route and these signs will take you from the previous junction, through Anstruther and on, back to the St Andrews linking section.

Don't forget to turn left for Kilrenny before the B9131 (interesting church). Cross the A917 to Cellardyke, passing a caravan site, then go on to Anstruther. Cellardyke harbour is

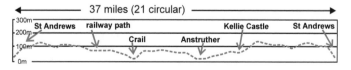

very pretty and you should stop and have a look. Between Cellardyke and Anstruther, the signed route runs near the shore and you should be sure to go that way to take in the old village houses.

Anstruther has a fisheries museum, a choice of eating places, a bike shop and a restored fishing boat. Leave Anstruther on the B9131 but turn left off it to farm tracks beyond the village. This is marked as a cycle route. The route climbs gently here, with views over the Forth to East Lothian. On the way, you can visit Kellie Castle (Scottish National Trust). It also has a beautiful garden and a tearoom. There are no refreshment facilities in Arncroach or Carnbee.

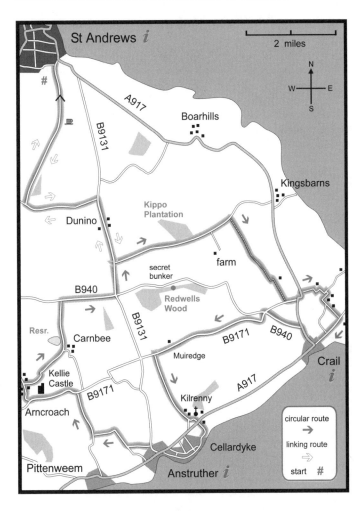

ST ANDREWS, TENTSMUIR FOREST AND THE FIRTH OF TAY

Sea views and forest, flat to Newport, hilly after that!
Route grading: **Varied** (30 miles)

The above distance is the circular part only. The leg from St Andrews is a further 6 miles each way. The cycle route from St Andrews to Guardbridge is now on the track bed of an old railway line. This is not difficult to find, as it begins from the 17th green just off Golf Place in St Andrews. The route is well signed.

The circular part of the route is signposted by Fife Cycleways as part of their Howe of Fife East route, with blue cycle signs. Between Guardbridge and Leuchars (train station) the route runs on a cyclepath. In Leuchars, it's on quiet streets then it heads out on small roads towards Tentsmuir Forest. In Leuchars, you will pass the twelfth-century parish church, with its round Roman-style arches.

Unlike most forests in Scotland, Tentsmuir Forest is flat. Kinshaldy Beach behind it is lovely and has a remote air, with the pines of the forest behind. However, this is sometimes disturbed by planes taking off from nearby RAF Leuchars. As indicated on the map, there are two different ways to go through the forest. The sea is not actually visible from the coastal route most of the time.

After Tentsmuir, the route is by the sea, passing through Tayport to Newport-on-Tay then Wormit. South of Wormit, you turn west off the B946 towards Balmerino Abbey (a ruin). The diversion to the abbey is a long descent and an equally long climb up. You can miss out this climb by going via Gauldry, which has a pub. Balmerino Abbey was founded in 1226, when Scotland became a Protestant country. Unfortunately, less of it remains than the ruined border abbeys.

The return leg via Balmullo is much hillier than the coastal section; there is virtually no flat on it. However, the

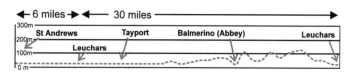

compensation for this are some good views.

St Andrews has one of the oldest universities in Britain, founded in 1411. The reflector telescope was invented here. Mary Queen of Scots planted a tree. The Treaty of Union between England and Scotland stipulates the university must never cease to function as such. The town is very well preserved and, of course, its golf club is recognised as the ruling body for the sport worldwide.

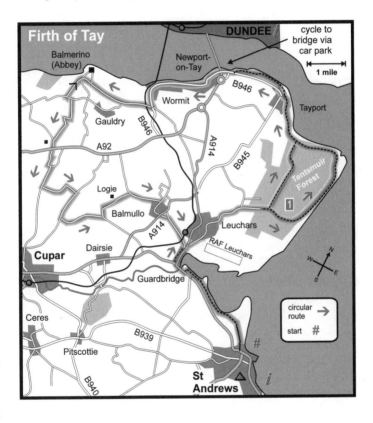

EDINBURGH TO THE FALKIRK WHEEL

On the Union Canal towpath*
Route grading: **Easy – any bike** (32 miles)
*For the other part of the Millennium Link (the canal
towpath route connecting Edinburgh to Glasgow), see
under Glasgow

You can join the towpath at any point, but in Edinburgh it starts
at Port Hopetoun, near Lothian Road. Originally the canal basin
here would have been piled with coal brought in by canal boat,
now it's the site of a leisure complex. You pass the Leamington
Lift Bridge then go past tenements to Harrison Park. Take care
at the narrow sections under the bridges. Shortly after this, you
go over the high aqueduct which carries the canal over the Water
of Leith (walk). The canal was broken at Wester Hailes but this
is now joined up again as part of the Millennium Link project.
After this, you pass over the dual carriageway city bypass and you
are in open countryside.

The Bridge Inn at Ratho is an obvious stop. If you want to
find food further on in Broxburn or Winchburgh, you will have
to leave the canal. At Linlithgow, the Canal Society provides boat
trips in the summer. There is a canal museum with a tearoom.

After Linlithgow, you pass over the Avon Aqueduct eighty-
six feet above the river. Approaching Falkirk, the route
becomes more urban again, but still attractive, with views of
back gardens. You have to pass through the Falkirk Tunnel.
This is 636 metres long and quite dark, so bike lights are
recommended. It's impossible to cycle but there is a handrail
to guide pedestrians. After this, there is blinding daylight
again and the Falkirk Wheel.

Coming from Edinburgh, the Wheel is visible some way off.
This rotary boat lift is unique in the world, and very impressive.
There is a restaurant, shop and visitor centre. Beyond the
Wheel, you can continue cycling west on the Forth–Clyde
Canal towpath to Glasgow (see under Glasgow). At the west
end of the Forth–Clyde Canal, it's also possible to cycle from
Bowling to Loch Lomond using the National Cycle Network –
see my book, *Scotland – the National Cycle Network*.

Please be considerate when cycling on canal towpaths.
Anglers, walkers and boaters use towpaths too. Warn others of
your approach, a polite 'hello' and 'thank you' mean a lot.

EDINBURGH TO THE FALKIRK WHEEL

Watch out for anglers' tackle and give them time to move it before you try to pass. If you have to cycle after dark, use lights. If you are organising a group cycle ride, you must apply to British Waterways for permission.

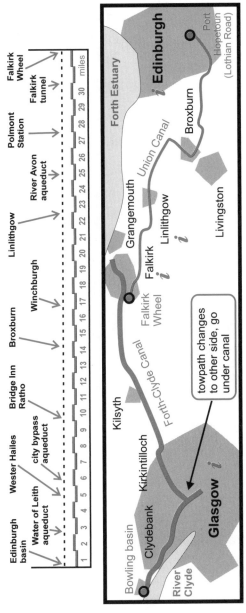

ROUTES FROM GLASGOW

DISTANCES AND ROUTE GRADING

CHAPTER 3

ROUTES FROM GLASGOW

This chapter describes routes within reach of Glasgow. It includes two routes which start from central Glasgow. The Glasgow to Loch Lomond route starts from near the Scottish Exhibition and Conference Centre (SECC) at Bell's Bridge. The 'art and the park' route is a short route mostly in public parks just south of this.

The Loch Lomond route is part of National Cycle Network Route 7. It can be extended further north via Drymen, and beyond that into the Highlands (see also Chapter 4).

Further west, two further routes are described. The Bridge of Weir route takes advantage of National Cycle Network Routes 7 and 75, creating a circular route by adding some quiet, if hilly, roads. The National Cycle Network routes are described in detail in my book: *Scotland – the National Cycle Network*. The Greenock Cut route is certainly hilly, but with great views and an interesting history.

The Forth–Clyde Canal towpath, which connects Edinburgh and Glasgow, is described as far as Falkirk. East of Falkirk, you can continue to Edinburgh on the Union Canal towpath. See the Edinburgh chapter (page 62).

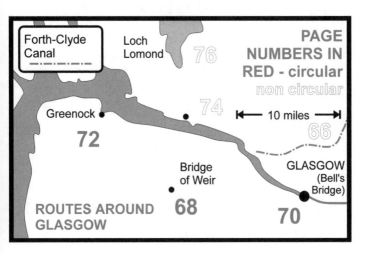

GLASGOW TO THE FALKIRK WHEEL

On the Forth–Clyde Canal towpath*
Route grading: **Easy – any bike** (34 miles)
*For the other part of the Millennium Link (the canal towpath route connecting Glasgow to Edinburgh), see under Edinburgh

The west end of the Forth–Clyde Canal is at Bowling, several miles west of Glasgow, by the River Clyde. You can start there, possibly getting the train to Bowling, or begin in Glasgow if you prefer.

The Maryhill locks near the River Kelvin are an interesting point to start. Note that the canal splits in two just east of this. A southern spur leads past Partick Thistle football ground. East of this junction, the canal towpath is on the north side, and west of this junction it's on the south side. To cross between the two towpaths, you have to pass under the canal on a busy road. You can avoid this by starting at Cadder Road or Possil Loch.

As you work east out of Glasgow, you pass golf courses and cemeteries then meet The Stables pub. This serves food all day and has tables outside. There's an urban · section in Kirkintilloch then the scenery becomes more attractive as you enter the Kelvin Valley. There are lots of mature trees, the Kilsyth Hills being visible to the north.

Unlike the Union Canal, the Forth–Clyde has locks which detain boats from time to time. Between Kirkintilloch and the Falkirk Wheel, you would have to leave the towpath to get food or drink.

Despite being very large, the Wheel is not visible as you approach it. This rotary boat lift is unique in the world, and very impressive. There is a restaurant, shop and visitor centre. You can continue cycling east on the Union Canal towpath to Edinburgh (see under Edinburgh). At the west end of the Forth–Clyde Canal, it's also possible to cycle from Bowling to Loch Lomond using the National Cycle Network – see my book: *Scotland – the National Cycle Network*.

Please be considerate to others when cycling on canal towpaths. Give way to people and warn them of your approach. Watch out for anglers' tackle and give them time to move it before you try to pass. If you have to cycle after dark, use lights. If you are organising a group cycle ride, you must apply to British Waterways for permission.

GLASGOW TO THE FALKIRK WHEEL

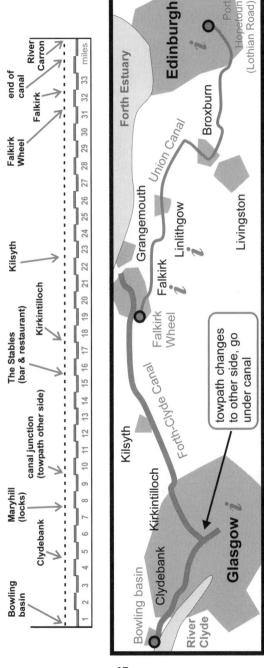

BRIDGE OF WEIR AND LOCHWINNOCH

Cyclepath and quiet roads
Route grading: **Easy – any bike** (15 miles)

This circular route is really a triangle. Two sides of the triangle are on cyclepaths, and the other is on quiet back roads. The route is on the fringe of the Glasgow conurbation, where the city streets turn into the rolling countryside of the Clyde Valley. It's convenient for Glasgow, while also providing some great views. The route is described starting from Bridge of Weir. To travel by train, start from Lochwinnoch, which has a train station nearby.

Join the cyclepath (National Route 75) in Bridge of Weir, near where it passes under the A761. An access point is by the Railway Tavern (Freeland Church and Post Office opposite). Turn right (west) onto the cyclepath and cycle for a very short distance to a steam-engine sculpture made out of a barrel. Immediately after this, turn left off the cyclepath – don't cross the bridge over the road.

Turn left onto the public road, then immediately sharp left up a steep hill (Horsewood Road). Keep straight on at the crossroads to enter Lawmarnock Road. You pass a golf course on the left. After that, keep straight on for two miles. Eventually you pass under two electricity lines. You have to take a right turn shortly after the second electricity line. This is a staggered junction, so be sure to take the first right, not the second. After this, there is a lovely rolling road with lots of descent and views of Castle Semple Loch.

Go straight over at the next crossroads then turn right at a T junction with a broken wall. Turn left at the B786, then left in Lochwinnoch, signed 'Castle Semple Country Park'. There is a visitor centre near where you enter the park, which has toilets and a tearoom. A short ramp leads from the park to the cyclepath. Cycle north-east, with the loch visible on your right. This section is a very gentle uphill on a tarmac surface.

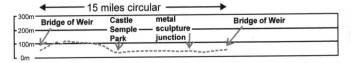

Initially, the path runs through woodland, but towards Kilbarchan the countryside becomes more open. You pass a small temple on a hill, which is not really a religious building. Kilbarchan is named after a sixth-century holy man: Barchan, the Kil part meaning 'church'. Kilbarchan was a weaving centre and the National Trust have a preserved weaver's cottage in the appropriately named Shuttle Street.

After Kilbarchan, the cyclepath crosses over the A737 then runs near it for a little way. There is a pelican crossing. Shortly after this, you come to a sculpture made of welded steel. This is intended to represent the aurora borealis. Here you have to turn left, leaving Route 7 and going onto Route 75. 'To Greenock' is painted on the ground and you should go that way. The other direction takes you to Bell's Bridge in central Glasgow via Paisley and various public parks (16 miles).

The final section is fairly flat, through attractive countryside. When you pass under the A761, you will be in Bridge of Weir.

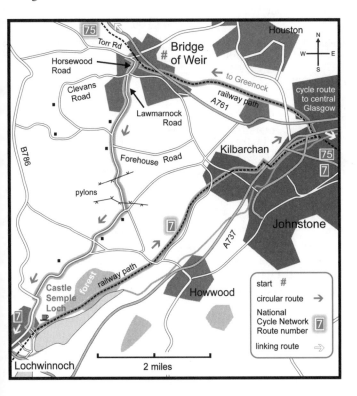

GLASGOW – ART AND THE PARK

Three parks, two art galleries, a swimming pool – and you get to ride your bike
Route grading: **Easy** (10 miles)

This short circular route will be interesting to visitors to Glasgow and families who are looking for a bike ride on their doorstep. Navigation in a city requires care. These notes supplement the maps. The route in Pollock Park is signed 'National Cycle Routes 7 and 75'. Between Ross Hall and Pollock Park, it's signed as a local cycle route.

Starting from Pollock Park, begin at the Dumbreck Road entrance, a light-controlled crossing leads across. A feature of Pollock Park is The Burrell Collection; this is housed in a new building opened in 1983.

West of the park, the route is on a cyclepath by White Cart Water. Reach this by going past Pollock House car park. Keep beside the river and follow bike signs for Paisley. After the park, use the footpath and a pelican crossing at a roundabout on Corkerhill Road. The route runs through housing estates near White Cart Water. After Linthaugh Road, cross over into Ross Hall Park on a footbridge near a nursery school. Turn right and go upstream after crossing the river.

Leave Ross Hall Park, with the river on your right, passing Ross Hall High School. The crossing to Cardonald Drive is via a footbridge. After this, you go round a bowling green, then, as you go along Dundee Drive near the railway, there's a rise then a descent.

Use the pelican crossing near Cardonald College. After crossing Corkerhill Road, go along Bellahouston Drive then cross Mosspark Boulevard to enter Bellahouston Park. Head towards the swimming pool. The route through Bellahouston Park is flat. Leave the park at the 'Dumbreck Road' entrance. Cross this using the light-controlled crossing, and the cycle route is on the other side.

After the 'Dumbreck Road' exit from Bellahouston Park, go

along Urrdale Road then turn left to cross the M8 motorway on a footbridge to Clifford Street, where you turn right.

To return to Pollock Park, turn right to another cyclepath part way along Clifford Street (entry via Kirkwood Street). After this, follow signs for Pollock Park and Paisley. The route to Pollock Park crosses back over the M8 and is mostly cyclepath, except where you cross over the M77 on Nithsdale Road, near Dumbreck train station. The cyclepath ends opposite the park.

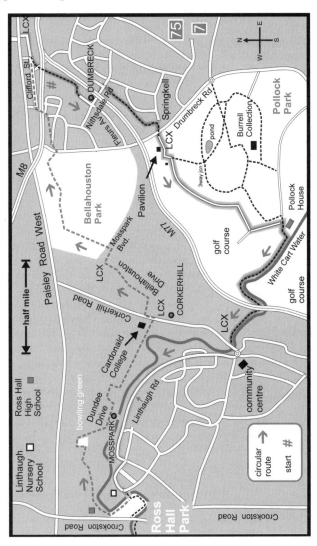

THE GREENOCK CUT AND OTHER TRACKS

An interesting day out – good views
Route grading: **Hilly – mountain bike** (20 miles)

This route is hilly but if you were to drive to the start and remain at high level, you could avoid the steepest hills. The Greenock Cut is a sort of mini-canal, built to provide drinking water and water power for Greenock. It was finished in 1827. The Cut powered 19 water wheels and provided 21,000 cubic feet of water a day. This cycle route follows the path beside it.

Reaching the Cut from Greenock is mostly a matter of going up the steepest hill. From Greenock Central train station (trains take bikes), go uphill, turn right then left (keep going uphill). Turn right, then left at the 'Old Largs' road sign. Follow a sign for the Cut, then turn left up a minor road (no sign). Do not go downhill at any time – if you get lost, ask someone.

There are views over the Firth of Clyde towards the Kyles of Bute and lots of minor roads and tracks to explore. There will be few cars. The Cut itself needs care, as the path is fairly narrow and there are gates to manoeuvre your bike through. The rest of the tracks are not gated.

Biking round anticlockwise will be slightly slower, as it's a gentle uphill. Going round clockwise can be faster but needs care, as the path is fairly narrow. The aqueduct cuts deeply into small gorges as it goes round the hill following the contour. These gorges are wooded. We met no pedestrians at all, except in the area of Cornalees Bridge Centre, and they'd all got there by car. You cross a minor road leading west from Loch Thom.

Once you've finished the Greenock Cut, you can do the Kelly Cut, or explore miles of tracks and minor roads around the various reservoirs. The Kelly Cut is an extension of the Greenock Cut. It was built in 1845 to increase the water supply. Construction is similar but the path is wider, if occasionally bumpy. The first 500m of the Kelly Cut forms part of a nature trail.

←——— 20 miles circular ———→

300m
200m Kelly Cut **Wemyss Bay**
          Inverkip   Loch Thom
Greenock Cut
0m

Things get steeper here if you follow the circular route marked on the map (actually a figure of eight). Take the track down the hill towards Wemyss Bay. You are losing height, which you will need to regain when you climb up again from Inverkip. If you are using the train, you could avoid this uphill climb by returning from Wemyss Bay station instead of Greenock. The route between Wemyss Bay and Inverkip is slightly more complex than can be displayed on the map here, and OS Landranger map 63 would be useful. As you will see from the map, the return to the start is on the quiet minor road to the east of Loch Thom.

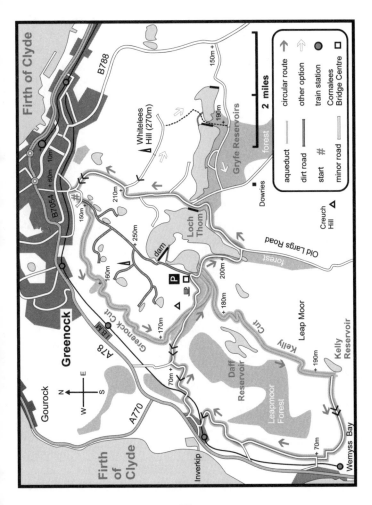

GLASGOW TO LOCH LOMOND

A signed route and away from traffic
Route grading: **Easy – any bike** (15 miles)

This route leads from Glasgow to Loch Lomond, now at the centre of Scotland's first National Park. The cycleway uses former railway lines, canal and riverside paths. It is the start of the National Cycle Network Lochs and Glens North Route 7. It also connects to routes described in the Central Highlands chapter of this book. Alternatively, you can hop on a train which will return you to Glasgow.

The route begins at Bell's Bridge, opposite the Scottish Exhibition and Conference Centre (SECC), by the River Clyde. Keep an eye out for the direction signs, though most of the time you'll be following a well-defined path. The instructions here will highlight where you might go wrong. Cycle downstream past the glass Moat House, then turn away from the river and cross over the Clydeside Expressway on a footbridge. The route is signposted but one thing that might lead you astray are the cycle signs leading to train stations. The Museum of Transport is shortly after the start, and has a tearoom. A further mile after this, you pass near Victoria Park and Fossil Grove.

At Clydebank, the route leaves the former railway and joins the Forth–Clyde Canal towpath. Shortly before this is a signed 'Route 7' section on a street by John Brown Engineering, then you see the blue and grey Playdrome building. Here you are directed by a pedestrian path to a pelican crossing. The canal is nearby. If you can't see it, look for a mock ocean liner (which is a fish restaurant). Cycle along the towpath, with the canal on your right.

After four miles, the towpath ends at Bowling. There's a bike shop here. The shop sells chocolate bars, etc. and if you become a customer they might even give you a coffee. Go under the railway bridge to have a look at the canal basin. The route continues over this bridge. It crosses a road, turning left into a park to follow an old railway line again. There is a further road crossing then you pass a Little Chef restaurant.

Towards Dumbarton, the railway line ends and you are on normal roads. These are well signed and take you through a public park, then into central Dumbarton. The route in Dumbarton takes you across the River Leven, immediately after which you turn sharp right into a public park. The sign is a bit faded. Where the path joins minor access roads, keep by the river. Eventually the river widens out into the loch. Tourist information, train station, boat trips, pubs and tearooms, it's all here. The cycle route continues through Loch Lomond Shores (a commercial development) to Balloch Castle Country Park, which has a view of the loch.

TRAIN STATIONS ON ROUTE

Exhibition Centre, Partick, Garscadden, Yoker, Clydebank, Singer, Dalmuir, Kilpatrick, Bowling, Dumbarton (East & Central), Renton, Alexandria and Balloch (Loch Lomond).

SPECIAL NOTE – Sustrans have advised that, in the medium term, the alignment of the first part of this route may possibly be changed. The changes would be between Bell's Bridge and Clydebank. They would, of course, be signed.

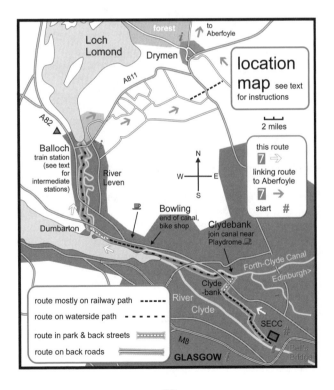

LOCH LOMOND TO ABERFOYLE

Into the Highlands from Loch Lomond
Route grading: **Hilly** (20 miles)

This is a continuation of the Glasgow to Loch Lomond cycle route. It is also part of National Cycle Network Route 7. It runs through farming country as far as Fintry, then crosses the Highland Boundary Fault.

The Glasgow to Loch Lomond section ends opposite Balloch tourist office, just after crossing the A811. From here, you are directed by footpaths and cycle lanes to Balloch Castle Country Park. The country park is a good spot for a picnic. The cycle route is signed. Take a right turn near the castle car park to find the exit to the A811. You are only on the A811 for about 50 metres, after which you turn right to a minor road – this is signposted.

Between the A811 and Drymen, the route follows a series of quiet minor roads. The Campsie Fells are visible to the east. Here the route is a gentle climb through cattle-farming country. Rob Roy used to rustle cattle here in the late seventeenth century, until eventually he became a legitimate cattle farmer himself.

As you ride north-east, you see a disused railway running near to the route. Shortly after the right turn for Croftamie, the route runs along it. It's broken by the A809, which you should take care in crossing. The route is carried over Endrick Water by a bridge which runs over a pipeline. After this, you turn left at a minor road and two miles after that you'll be in Drymen.

Drymen has a choice of pubs and places to eat. There is also a good choice of B&Bs and hotels. The village is also a major stopping point for those doing the long distance walk, the West Highland Way. This runs up the east shore of Loch Lomond; you can go as far as Rowardennan on a bike but after that you'd have to carry it. Leave Drymen on the minor road that passes by the side of the Clachan Inn. If in doubt, look for

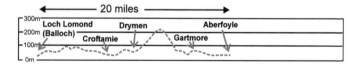

the steepest hill around – that's the one you're cycling up!

The hill out of Drymen is pretty unrelenting. Stopping on the way up not only gives you a rest but great views of Loch Lomond behind. The Fintry Hills are on the right and Loch Ard Forest on the left, as you get to the top of the hill. It's possible to get to Aberfoyle by cycling on the forest mountain bike routes, though this is not recommended if you have a lot of luggage.

The entry point to the forest routes is by a sign: Drymen Road, next to a forest car park. The National Cycle Network Route 7 takes you on minor roads through the village of Gartmore. Shortly after this, another converted railway line avoids the A81 and takes you directly into the centre of Aberfoyle. There is a good choice of B&Bs, hotels, tearooms, etc.

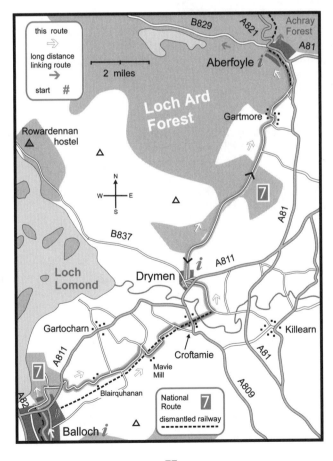

CENTRAL HIGHLANDS

DISTANCES AND ROUTE GRADING

CHAPTER 4

CENTRAL HIGHLANDS

The area covered in this chapter is mainland Scotland, roughly between the Highland Boundary Fault and the Great Glen. This area contains plenty of mountain scenery but also some busy roads. This chapter tells you how to enjoy the scenery but miss out the traffic. Many of the lochs and glens have roads on both sides, and often one side is much quieter. In some areas, for example the Angus Glens, there are lots of quiet roads where you can enjoy highland scenery without too many cars.

The Highlands are one area where the National Cycle Network has improved matters by introducing cyclepaths avoiding main roads. The routes in this book are different but they use parts of the Cycle Network occasionally.

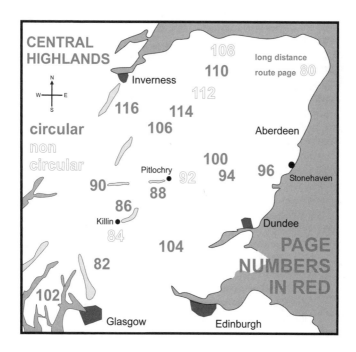

GLASGOW TO STONEHAVEN

A 182-mile coast to coast by the mountains and lochs of
the Central Highlands
Route grading: **Varied** (182 miles)

The long distance route described here consists of eight
circular day rides (red on map) that can be linked up to form a
week-long tour. The route between Glasgow and Aberfoyle is
described in the Glasgow chapter (pp 74–77), and the
remainder is in the following pages.

This area includes plenty of mountain scenery and also
some of the most famous lochs in Scotland. You'll not be
surprised to hear it also has some busy roads. You won't be
seeing much of them, though, because our route uses a
mixture of specially-built cyclepaths and quiet minor roads.

The prevailing wind is from the west so if you are doing the
whole thing it might be sensible to start from Aberfoyle or
Glasgow, rather than Stonehaven. There are train stations at
Glasgow, Pitlochry and Stonehaven.

The early part of the route between Aberfoyle and
Callander takes in lovely Loch Katrine and some of it is on the
water board road (no cars). Between Loch Katrine and
Callander, the greater part of the route is on cyclepath.

Between Callander and Killin, the route uses part of the
National Cycle Network Route 7. This is mostly specially-built
cyclepath. It follows the route of an old railway line, going over
an impressive viaduct in Glen Ogle. The descent to Killin is
through Acharn Forest, with fine views of Loch Tay.

Between Killin and Pitlochry, the route uses roads on the
south side of the lochs, too narrow for the tourist coaches but
ideal for cycling. Side trips are also possible, taking in lovely
Glen Lyon and quiet Loch Rannoch, with its native pine
forests.

Between Pitlochry and Kirkmichael, there is a big hill then
the scenery changes. Quiet glens run deep into the Grampian
Mountains. The towns of Alyth, Kirriemuir and Stonehaven
are interesting, with small stone-built closes and people with
time to talk.

Most of the towns and villages on the route are well served
by B&Bs, hotels, youth hostels and bunkhouses so there are
plenty of places to stay. There's also lots of historic interest. If

you cycle round Loch Katrine, you'll pass Glengyle, the birth-place of Rob Roy MacGregor.

Kirriemuir is the birthplace of James Barrie, creator of Peter Pan, and more recently Bon Scott, lead singer of AC/DC. Spectacular Dunnottar Castle (which is pictured on the front cover) near Stonehaven is at the end of the route, just south of Aberdeen.

There are plenty of circular day rides in the detailed maps. If you are doing the whole thing, and using the train to start or finish, reserve a place for your bike, as spaces for bikes on trains are limited.

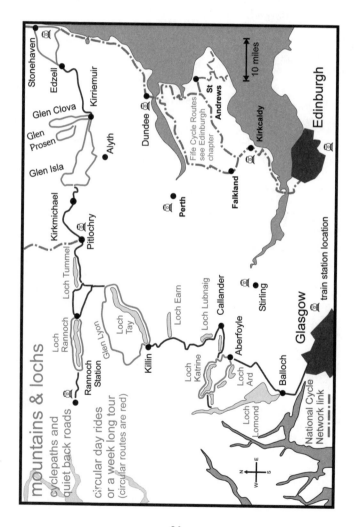

ABERFOYLE TO LOCH KATRINE

Begins very easily – no cars for 13 miles
Route grading: **Hilly** (30 miles)

The water board road by Loch Katrine has the unique feature that it has no cars; bikes, however, are allowed. Add to this that it is one of the loveliest roads in Britain and you have 13 miles of pure delight. The circular route is via Lochs Arklet, Chon and Ard – on normal roads this time but still attractive. The pleasure steamer S.S. *Sir Walter Scott* sails on Loch Katrine, and combined cycle rides and steamboat sailings are possible.

Loch Katrine is 10 miles long and was the inspiration for Sir Walter Scott's *The Lady of the Lake.* Glengyle (see map) is the birthplace of the outlaw or hero Rob Roy MacGregor. Loch Katrine has provided a water supply for Glasgow since 1859.

Start at Trossachs Pier, from where the steamer S.S. *Sir Walter Scott* sails. The road winds through trees close to the loch shore. Do not forget the possibility of the odd water board Land Rover on the road, not to mention some very complacent sheep.

Just over a quarter of the way round, you might have the illusion that you are halfway along, as the pier and house at Stronachlachar seem quite close. You realise that this is plainly not so at the top of a steady climb which follows, as the tail of the loch curves round to the north-west. Also visible to the west is Loch Arklet. The hills in the distance are on the far side of Loch Lomond. Stronachlachar Pier has toilets and shelter from any rain but little else. A possible diversion might be to the Inversnaid Hotel on Loch Lomond for a bar lunch.

The road to Aberfoyle is mainly downhill once you have climbed up to the T junction by Loch Arklet. There is some up and down by Loch Chon. After this, there is a slight climb, then a descent to enter Aberfoyle. Liz MacGregor's tearoom on the corner is recommended. Aberfoyle has a tourist office, B&Bs, hotels and shops, some providing carry-out food.

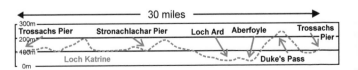

If you have left a car at the Trossachs Pier, you will have to return to it via the Duke's Pass, four more miles and a climb of 210 metres – good views, though. The route to Callander is on forest trails, see map below for entry point.

STEAMBOAT SAILINGS

The S.S. *Sir Walter Scott*, which sails on Loch Katrine, was built by Wm. Denny at Dumbarton and taken in sections up Loch Lomond by barge in 1899, then hauled up by horse and cart from Inversnaid. Sailing times from Trossachs Pier: 11.00 a.m., 1.45 p.m., 3.15 p.m. From Stronachlachar: 12 noon only. Enquiries to: 01877 376316. Cycle hire from the pier.

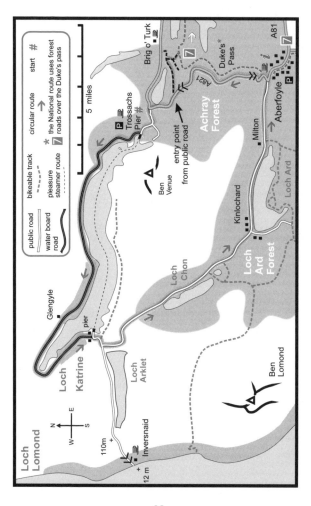

LOCH VENACHAR, CALLANDER AND KILLIN

A former railway, mainly easy, great scenery
Route grading: **Varied – any bike** (35 miles)

Most of this is on a converted railway line. The gradients are mostly gentle, though there are a few short steep sections. Watch out particularly for the zigzags near Loch Earn.

Coming from Aberfoyle on the public road, you will have climbed over the Duke's Pass and descended to Loch Achray. Access to the trail on the south side of Lochs Achray and Venachar is through a stone-built vehicle barrier just south of Loch Achray at the bottom of the hill (see map previous page). The route follows a trail through the woods. Turn right just before a farmhouse. Apart from that, turn left at every junction.

Halfway along Loch Venachar, you meet a public road. Keep straight on into Callander, passing a hostel and bike hirer (see red triangle on map). In Callander, turn left, then left again at the traffic lights. Callander has hotels, shops, tearooms and a large number of carry-out food places. The Rob Roy Centre shares an old church building with the tourist office in the centre.

Continuing north, you can avoid Main Street in Callander by following the cycle route signs after you cross the bridge over the River Teith. If you are parking a car in Callander, the car park is by the Dreadnought Hotel, which is unmistakable. Entry to the cycle route going north is about 100 metres north of the Dreadnought Hotel on the left.

South of the A821, the route passes through a park by the river. North of this, it is on the railway line for the first mile. The railway once crossed the river after this, but the bridge is missing so the bike route continues on the west bank of the river until Loch Lubnaig. There are eating places in Strathyre, plus a shop.

North of Strathyre, the route is on a minor road to Balquhidder. Rob Roy's grave is at the little churchyard here. Following this, the route over Glen Ogle is on the former

35 miles

300m
Trossachs Pier
200m **(Loch Katrine)**   Callander   Strathyre   Glen Ogle →
100m
Loch Achray   Loch Venachar   Acharn Forest   Killin
0m

railway line. This includes an impressive viaduct high above the main road. Just before Killin, the route passes through Acharn Forest. The top section is steep. Killin is about the same size as Callander and has many facilities, including a youth hostel and a tourist office. There's an outdoor shop which hires bikes and carries some spare parts.

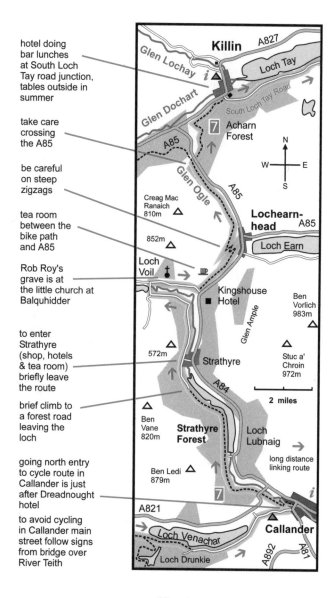

hotel doing bar lunches at South Loch Tay road junction, tables outside in summer

take care crossing the A85

be careful on steep zigzags

tea room between the bike path and A85

Rob Roy's grave is at the little church at Balquhidder

to enter Strathyre (shop, hotels & tea room) briefly leave the route

brief climb to a forest road leaving the loch

going north entry to cycle route in Callander is just after Dreadnought hotel

to avoid cycling in Callander main street follow signs from bridge over River Teith

GLEN LYON AND LOCH TAY

Challenging hills, fast descents, big mountains
Route grading: **Hilly** (58 miles)

This is a good route for experienced cyclists, as it combines quiet roads with some of the best scenery in Scotland. It is best done clockwise because the steep Ben Heasgarnich descent is straight on the north side.

Cycle north out of Killin, then take the first turning on the left just before the bridge over the River Lochay. The first nine miles is a gentle ascent, hardly noticeable really, giving you no indication at all of the climb ahead. The River Lochay is very pretty. You will meet cattle on the road and hillwalkers' cars.

Most people walk up at least part of the steep climb on the hydro-power road. There are several very tight bends. If there has been recent rain, debris from the hill may be washed onto the road. There will be cattle. The top is undulating, then it's a straight descent down to Glen Lyon.

The road down Glen Lyon is mostly a gentle descent. Glen Lyon is the longest glen in Scotland and one of the prettiest. As you ride down, you get fine views. The Post Office and shop at Bridge of Balgie is also a tearoom. After Bridge of Balgie, it's a cruise, with only a small uphill section just before Fortingall. The Fortingall Hotel does cream teas on the lawn outside, if the weather is sunny. Fortingall is known for the ancient yew tree in the churchyard, which may be over 2,000 years old.

After Fortingall, you pass a blacksmith's shop near Coshieville, briefly turning right onto the B846 before crossing the River Lyon again to get to Kenmore. The signposted National Cycle Route 7 continues east to Weem on the B846.

Kenmore is quite a small place. It has a food shop, a tearoom, a hotel and several B&Bs. A mile further on, the Croft na Caber water sports centre on the south Loch Tay road has a café. Also next to Croft na Caber is the Scottish Crannog Centre: a reproduction crannog by Edinburgh University.

There were crannogs at one time in lochs all over Scotland. Crannogs are settlements on water, erected on stilts. Presumably, in uncertain times, their isolation from the mainland offered a measure of defence from attack. Apart from this one, they all date from 2,000 years ago or more.

GLEN LYON AND LOCH TAY

As you cycle towards Killin, on the other side of Loch Tay, you'll see the Ben Lawers range, some of the grandest mountains in Scotland: Meall nan Tarmachan, which towers over Killin; Ben Lawers and Meall Garbh further east.

The Ardeonaig Hotel, roughly halfway along the loch, does beautiful food. No doubt they could also produce coffee and shortbread.

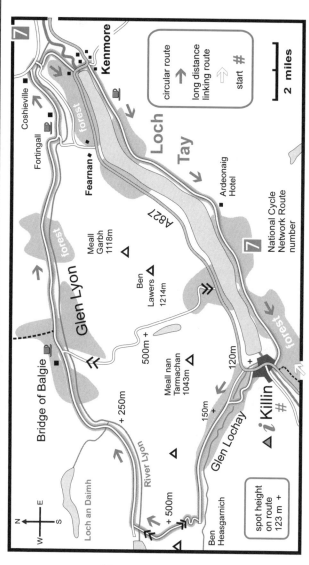

Killin · Ardeonaig · Kenmore · Fortingall · Bridge of Balgie · Killin

400m · 300m · 200m · 100m

hydro power road

58 miles circular

Kenmore

circular route
long distance linking route
start #

2 miles

Loch Tay

Coshieville

Fortingall

Fearnan

· Ardeonaig Hotel

forest

Glen Lyon forest

Meall Garbh 1118m △

Ben Lawers 1214m △

National Cycle Network Route number

7

Bridge of Balgie

500m +

Meall nan Tarmachan 1043m △

120m

forest

150m +

Killin △ i #

+ 250m

△

Glen Lochay

River Lyon

+ 500m

Ben Heasgarnich

Loch an Daimh

△

spot height on route 123 m +

N · E · W · S

87

LOCH TUMMEL AND STRATH TAY

Following the loch and the River Tay
Route grading: **Varied** (37 miles)

This is a lovely route with one big hill. The description here is from Pitlochry. The southern part of the route is also National Cycle Network Route 7.

Start from the A9 access road to Pitlochry Festival Theatre, which is on the west side of the River Tummel. You can get to it from the town by following walking signs for the theatre and crossing the River Tummel on a footbridge. Alternatively, leave the town on Atholl Road (the main street), cycling south. Turn right immediately after going under a curved arch railway bridge, and bear right at the next junction.

From the theatre, cycle up the hill to the main A9. On the north side of the slip road is a footpath signposted 'Loch Faskally Walk'. This leads to a grass area beside the main road, which you should cycle along. After a little way, turn left through a gate, then continue in the same direction to an underpass taking you under the A9. You are now on the south Loch Tummel road.

The road winds prettily alongside the river, arriving at Loch Tummel after a few hills. When you reach the other end of the loch, turn left onto the B846 to cross over to Strath Tay.

Between Coshieville and Logierait, the road follows the River Tay downstream. There is a hotel at Weem and before that you pass Castle Menzies. Aberfeldy is less than a mile off-route. It has lots of facilities, but no bike shop. There is a food shop in Strath Tay village, just north of Grandtully.

A mile after Strath Tay village, you briefly join the A827, turning right onto it to cross the river to get to the B898. Three miles on from this, you need to cross the former railway bridge at Logierait. This is not visible but it is signed from both directions. At the south end, you join the track to it near a stone cottage with two chimneys.

After crossing the bridge, turn sharp left, then turn right up

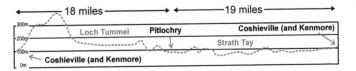

a hill near the Logierait Hotel. After this, continue for four miles to enter Pitlochry.

Pitlochry seems at first glance to be a seaside resort marooned in the middle of the Highlands, but it has plenty of charms. The pub at Moulin is worth a visit and there are lots of peaceful walks by the River Tummel for the evening. There is a good bike shop, a youth hostel, a backpackers' hostel, lots of hotels and B&Bs, and a campsite. There's also a distillery, a gem factory, a fish ladder and Pitlochry Festival Theatre.

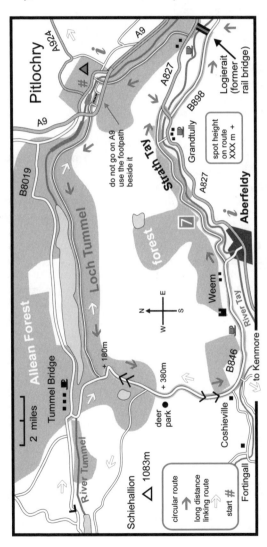

AROUND LOCH RANNOCH

An easy cycle round an attractive loch
Route grading: **Easy** (22 miles)

This is a very easy cycle round a typical Highland loch. The hills are at the west end and these are very slight. There are sandy beaches on the north shore at the west end of the loch and the pebble beach just south of Kinloch Rannoch is very attractive, with views of the mountains the other side of Rannoch Moor.

There is quite a lot of natural Scots pine forest in the vicinity of Loch Rannoch. You actually cycle through the Black Wood of Rannoch while going round but there are more pine woods on the hills to the south. Forest trails lead up from Carie and you can bike some of these. There's a food shop in Kinloch Rannoch, and the Dunalistair Hotel in the square has tables outside, where you can take your meal or drinks. There is also a time-share establishment and hotel just west of Kinloch Rannoch, which can provide food. For an update on the latest situation regarding accommodation and facilities in the area, see www.rannoch.net.

Rannoch station, the remotest railway station in Britain, is four miles further west. There's a tearoom in the station and a hotel nearby, which also does bar food. Cycling to it will involve a bit of a climb. You can't go any further than that unless you take a train on the West Highland Line (to Glasgow or Fort William). Another possible option for refreshments is Talladh-A-Bheithe Lodge on the north shore of the Loch. This establishment is run by a German family and offers excellent home baking, as well as full meals and accommodation.

Schiehallion, the mountain that overlooks the loch, was the subject of a famous experiment by Maskelyne, the Astronomer Royal. The intention was to determine the mass of the Earth by observing the deflection of a pendulum caused by the mass of the mountain itself. Schiehallion was considered suitable because of its isolated position and large size.

The school marked on the map is Rannoch School, which is

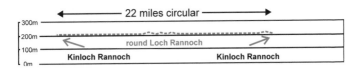

a private fee-paying establishment with an outdoor ethos. At the time of writing, it was about to close. The Rannoch area has a history of cattle-thieving and many Highlanders were hung by government troops, as they attempted to gain control of the lawless clans. Of these, the Macgregors were the fiercest, stealing cattle from miles around and driving them into Rannoch. The Black Wood of Rannoch is one of the remaining areas of the original Caledonian Pine Forest that once covered the whole of Scotland.

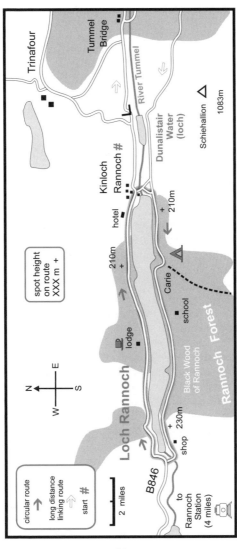

PITLOCHRY TO GLEN ISLA

A linking section – not circular
Route grading: **Hilly** (18 miles)

This is a long climb coming out of Pitlochry but it's mostly steady rather than steep. There is one short steep part just after a left bend (double arrows on map). Climbing up, you'll see Pitlochry's local mountain on the left, Ben Vrackie.

The road is unfenced and there will probably be sheep wandering about. Despite the fact that it is a class A road, it is normally reasonably quiet, as we are leaving the popular tourist areas.

As you come up the A924, you pass a bike shop in Pitlochry then, shortly after, the Moulin Hotel, which is a great local pub full of character. After that, there are no refreshment stops until Kirkmichael. This road is really skirting the southern edge of the Grampian and Cairngorm Mountains. This is the largest upland area in Scotland, containing 39 separate summits (Munros) over 3,000 feet.

Once the climb is done, it's virtually all downhill until you get to Kirkmichael. There are several B&Bs, some in Kirkmichael and some you'll pass by just north of the village. There's a food shop and café in the local garage. Just after that, at the south side of the village at the B950 road junction, the Strathardle Inn does excellent food and has real ale. The Kirkmichael Hotel was closed but has recently reopened. There is another hotel, The Log Cabin, just west of the village; this is a Norwegian-style building in a rural setting.

Continuing east, there's a brief climb out of Kirkmichael then a flatter section before reaching Dalrulzion. The hotel there is just north of the road junction and can provide just a cup of tea or full board and accommodation.

The section north of Dalrulzion, leading to Glen Isla, is described on the next page. As indicated on the map, don't forget to turn off the A93 at the sign for Drumore or you'll end up in Braemar.

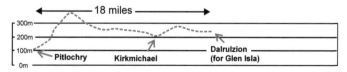

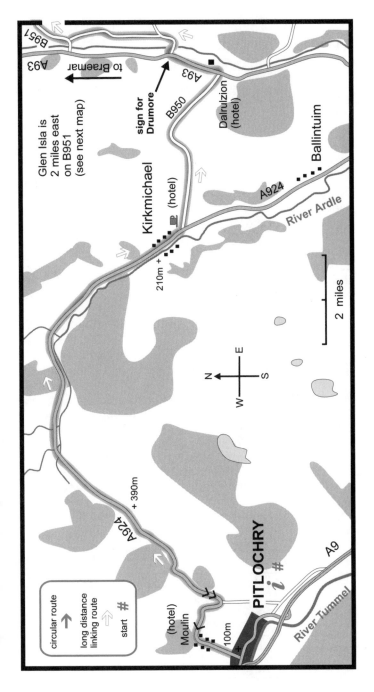

B951

A93

to Braemar

A93

sign for
Drumore

B950

Dalrulzion
(hotel)

Glen Isla is
2 miles east
on B951
(see next map)

Kirkmichael

Ballintuim

(hotel)

A924

River Ardle

210m +

2 miles

N
W — E
S

A924 + 390m

PITLOCHRY
i #

A9

(hotel)
Moulin

100m

River Tummel

circular route

long distance
linking route

start #

GLEN ISLA TO KIRRIEMUIR

Quiet glens, hills and forests
Route grading: **Hilly** (42 miles)

Not many people seem to know about Glen Isla, which is nice if you want to go cycling, but perhaps not so good if you are running a hotel. The area has a quiet charm. The Glens (Isla, Prosen, Clova and Esk) are known as the Angus Glens. The upper reaches, where they run deeply into the Grampian Mountains, are beautiful. Lower down, it's farms and woodland, with the minor roads usually quite quiet.

Going from Kirriemuir via Reekie Linn is hilly, so if this puts you off, you might consider going out and returning via Kirkton of Glenisla. Leave Kirriemuir on the B951. To get to this from the town centre, follow signs for 'The Glens' but keep on the A926, taking the turning after The Glens road (i.e. B951, not the B955).

Keep on the B951 for three miles until you reach Kirkton of Kingoldrum. The B951 does a sharp zigzag here. After this, turn left, then immediately right. If you are in any doubt, you should be going up the steep hill. After the climb, there's a long descent for two miles. You cross the river Melgam Water. Half a mile after that, bear right for Bridgend of Lintrathen. Turn left when you get to the loch. Bear right at the next junction, then keep on for just over a mile to the B954.

Just before the B954 junction, you pass Peel Farm, which has a tearoom. There are also deer, horses, goats, rabbits and sheep to look at. Shortly after joining the B954, you pass Reekie Linn, a good picnic spot with a waterfall. After crossing the River Isla, take the first right opposite Craigisla House. This starts with a gentle climb, becoming steeper and rising to 400 metres.

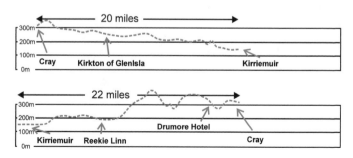

There's a descent to Brewlands Bridge. At the bottom of the hill, remember to turn left before you get to the bridge.

The road to Cray has another climb. Turn right a mile after Drumore Loch, then right a mile after that. Going east from Cray, it's mainly downhill. Kirkton of Glenisla has two hotels. After Glen Isla, there are no more food stops until Kirriemuir, but you could make a diversion to Peel Farm again without too much trouble.

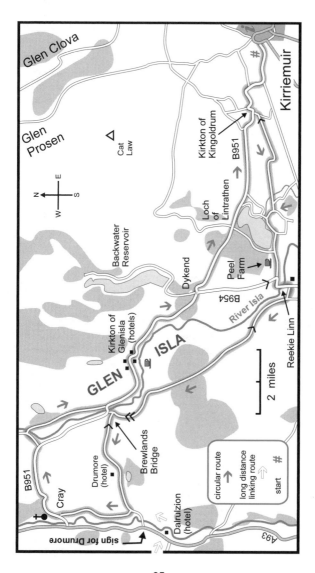

KIRRIEMUIR TO DUNNOTTAR CASTLE

Steep-sided glens and rolling country
Route grading: **Varied** (47 miles)

This is both a circular route and the final part of the
'Mountains and Lochs' long distance route. It is described
starting from Kirriemuir, so this includes a non-circular part.

Here the eastern edges of the Grampian Mountains
approach the sea. This is a low rainfall area but easterly winds
can bring a sea mist called *haar* in springtime. Kirriemuir is an
interesting town, full of winding streets and narrow stone-
built closes. James Barrie, author of *Peter Pan*, was born here,
also Bon Scott, lead singer of AC/DC.

Leave Kirriemuir, cycling north on the B955, following
signs for 'The Glens'. Keep on the B955 until you have
crossed the River South Esk, then turn right in a wooded area,
signed 'Edzell/Brechin'. You pass Cortachy Castle then climb
a hill. Bear right at the top for Memus. In Memus, turn right
then left at the phone box, following signs for Edzell. There's
a pub which does bar food slightly off-route (Drover's Inn, just
south of this junction).

From the Memus junction, generally keep straight on east,
through Fern to Tigerton. The road runs close to the edge of
the hills, giving views over the Angus countryside. Bear left in
Tigerton to climb out of the village. Keep straight on at the
next crossroads, then turn right and then left at the staggered
junction. A mile after this, you meet the B966 running into
Edzell. Turn left and under the arch to enter the town.

Edzell is a small town with several hotels, B&Bs and
tearooms. Edzell Castle is near. Cycling up Glen Esk is an
attractive ride and not particularly hilly, and Invermark Castle
is at the top of the Glen. To continue to Fettercairn, keep on
the B966. Fettercairn is smaller than Edzell.

Leave Fettercairn on the B974 towards Cairn o' Mount.
Keep on this for four miles until Clatterin' Brig (restaurant).
Here the B974 begins its serious climb to 455 metres at Cairn
o' Mount. We turn off it, turning right to cross the bridge,
then climb towards Auchenblae. The Cairn o' Mount road is
popular with motorcyclists in summer and may be snowbound
in winter.

After a climb, the road to Auchenblae levels off and runs

ABOVE: On the Old Edinburgh Road (page 18) (© Harry Henniker)

BELOW: Scott's View, River Tweed (page 36) (© Harry Henniker)

ABOVE: Firth   of Tay, winter's day (page 60) (© Harry Henniker)

BELOW: Author and swans, Union Canal towpath (page 62) (© Dave McArthur)

ABOVE: Falkirk Wheel (page 66) (© Harry Henniker)

BELOW: Crossing the loch (page 82) (© Harry Henniker)

ABOVE: Cruising down Glen Lyon (page 86) (© Harry Henniker)

BELOW: South Loch Tay Road (page 86) (© Harry Henniker)

Cycling picnic at Invermark Castle (page 96)
(© Harry Henniker)

ABOVE: B&B departure (page 108) (© Harry Henniker)

BELOW: Ardgour by Loch Linnhe (page 120) (© Harry Henniker)

ABOVE: Cruising down to Applecross (page 122) (© Harry Henniker)

BELOW: View to Suilven from near Ledmore (page 132) (© Harry Henniker)

ABOVE: Isle of Islay from Jura (page 156) (© Elaine Abbot)

BELOW: Keep your cycling helmet on in a broch! (page 192) (© Harry Henniker)

KIRRIEMUIR TO DUNNOTTAR CASTLE

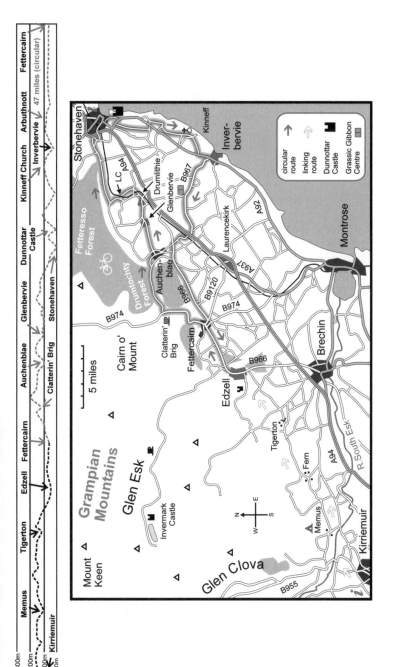

through lovely Strath Finella. Bear left towards the end of this wooded section (no sign) for Auchenblae. In Auchenblae, follow signs for Glenbervie and Drumlithie.

In Drumlithie, bear left at the pub (closed daytime), under the railway then descend steeply to a level crossing. Turn right after this. You pass Connachie Farm (cows crossing), then turn right at a T junction for a rolling descent towards Stonehaven. After five miles on this road, turn right at a water authority store then take the second left, which will take you to an overpass crossing the A92 to Stonehaven. Stonehaven has many attractions and an interesting harbour.

To continue from Stonehaven to Dunnottar Castle and beyond, leave Stonehaven going south on the A957. However, before you have left the town, you'll see a small one-way road leading off to the left. This will be signed 'National Cycle Network Route 1'. It leads steeply up a hill, leading to the sea-cliffs next to Dunnottar Castle. The castle (which is pictured on the front cover) is in a spectacular location, and looks quite ruined from the shore, but there is a lot to see inside – no tearoom, however.

South from the castle, you follow the Route 1 signs. This route follows Route 1, but leaves it just before Inverbervie. The National Route continues south to Montrose. Shortly before Inverbervie, you pass near the Old Church of Kinneff, where the crown of Scotland was hidden under the flagstones. Inverbervie has B&Bs, shops and a café but this route turns east to follow the B967 to Arbuthnott just before the town. You have a short distance on the A92, before turning right to the B967. This is a descent so you'll only be on it for a minute or two – look behind you and signal clearly when turning right.

Inland on the B967 is the Lewis Grassic Gibbon Centre. This is the Howe of the Mearns, difficult farming country made famous by James Leslie Mitchell. Even if you are not of a literary bent, the associated tearoom might attract you. After this, you have to cross the A94 to Fordoun. Remember to turn left to cross over the railway in the village. Shortly after that, you meet the B966, where you turn left, and not too long after that you'll be in Fettercairn. Edzell, with its tearooms, castle and hotels, is five miles to the east.

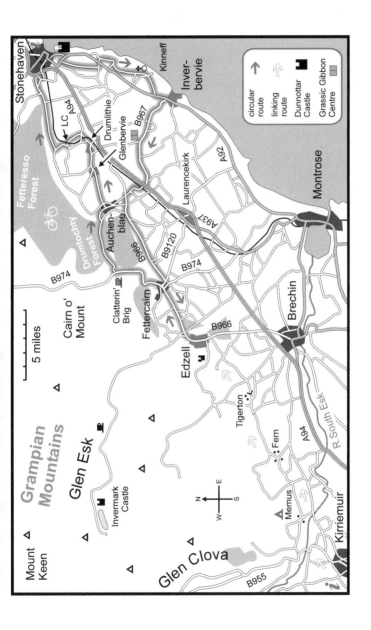

GLEN CLOVA AND GLEN PROSEN

Quiet glens cut deeply into the Grampian Mountains
Route grading: **Varied** (32 miles)
With Glen Prosen included: **Hilly** (44 miles)

In Kirriemuir, follow signs for 'The Glens' to the B955, then follow signs for Glen Clova. If you are taking in Glen Prosen as well, note that the Glen Prosen road is a left turn off the B955 in a wood just before you cross over the river Prosen Water (Prosen Bridge).

Glen Prosen is lovely but very hilly. There is a shop and a tearoom in the village. It will take a while to get round Glen Prosen, even if you don't linger in the tearoom. Eventually, you come out at Dykehead, where there is a hotel. You might like to walk up to the Airlie Memorial, which is near Dykehead (access from the Prosen road). This is worth a look, as the view of the surrounding hills and glens is superb.

Between Dykehead and the Clova Hotel there are no particularly big hills, rather a series of ups and downs. Like Glen Prosen, Glen Clova has two roads running up it. Going north on the west side of the glen is recommended, as you get a better view of the mountains.

The Clova Hotel has a climbers' bar at the back, as well as a normal lounge bar at the front. I prefer the climbers' bar, as it has an open fire and interesting climbing photos on the wall. Food is available all day and the hotel also has a bunkhouse, if you are looking for economical accommodation. Unfortunately, the youth hostel further up at Glen Doll closed in January 2002.

Riding up the glen a little further to the end of the public road at Glen Doll is highly recommended, as the scenery is quite special. The ride back to Kirriemuir has some hills too but you'll get back fairly quickly.

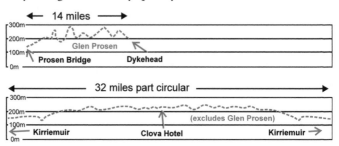

Kirriemuir is the birthplace of James Barrie, creator of *Peter Pan*. Even if you've only seen the Disney version, you should make an effort to see where he lived and the outside wash house that was his first theatre. On Barrie's death in 1937, there was a move to dismantle his house and re-erect it in the USA. Fortunately, this came to nothing and it is now owned by the National Trust.

Kirriemuir has a number of hotels and tearooms for refreshment; the Pilgrims tearoom is recommended. The town, with its narrow closes and streets, is quite interesting.

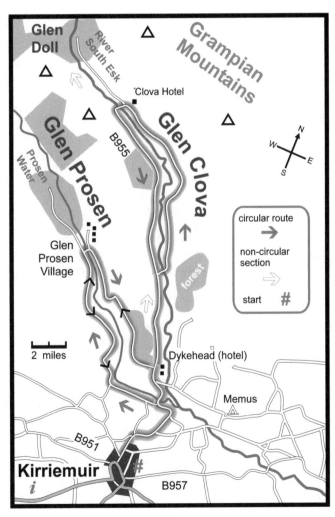

BUTE AND COWAL

A surprisingly quiet two-day ride
Route grading: **Hilly** (82 miles)

This is a circular weekend ride (train from Glasgow Central).
From Wemyss Bay, catch the Cal-Mac ferry to Rothesay, on
the island of Bute. Rothesay has a nostalgic air, the days of
trippers from Glasgow going doon the water being long past.
Bute Museum in Stuart Street is worth visiting, as is Mount
Stuart (see map).

In Rothesay, bike south on the B811 (past the hospital),
then get to Port Bannatyne by travelling north on the west-
coast road. This gives dramatic views of Arran. There is a café
at Ettrick Bay. Turn left to a track crossing the bay after a sign:
'Largievrechtan'. The ferry at Colintraive is a five-minute
crossing. The hotel on the Colintraive side does bar lunches.

Fork left just after Colintraive, to go by the sea on the B866.
Shortly after this, turn left on to the A8003, to go south
towards Tighnabruaich. There is a stiff climb, then a
spectacular view of the Kyles of Bute, then a descent to
Tighnabruaich. There are several hotels and B&Bs. If you
have enough energy, the minor road which loops south from
here (see map) is worth cycling.

Climb steeply out of Tighnabruaich and head north for
Otter Ferry. There is a hotel at Kilfinan, and The
Oystercatcher Restaurant and a food shop at Otter Ferry. The
next section is never long enough for me. It is one of the
loveliest rides in Scotland – flat, hardly any cars, the wind
usually behind you. You sail along in beautiful scenery, past
long shingle beaches.

This flat section ends just south of Newton, where you

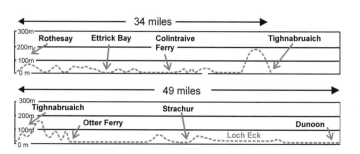

leave the sea, climbing inland. Turn left to the A886 near Newton, to continue north to Strachur. A shop at Strachur, just before the road junction, has a tearoom with tables outside. There is also a pub (see map).

The next section is south, past Loch Eck. At Strachur, turn right to the A815. At Loch Eck, you can cycle on the A815, or use a forest road on the west side (see map). Loch Eck contains freshwater herring which were marooned in the loch when it was cut off from the sea.

The Younger Botanic Garden has a tearoom. At Dunoon, use the coast road for the ferry. Note Western Ferries and Caledonian MacBrayne both operate ferries from Dunoon to Gourock, and all the terminal points differ.

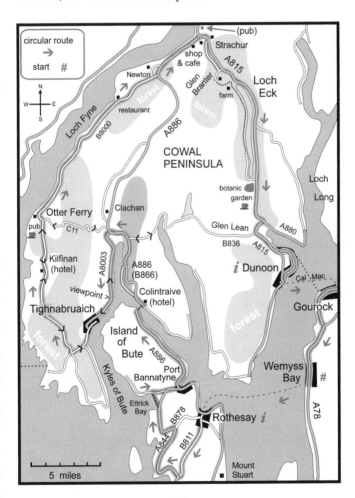

DUNNING AND STRATH EARN

Woods and farms, mountain views
Route grading: **Varied** (40 miles)

The peaceful village of Dunning is the centre of this route. It has an inn with a beer garden and a historic church.

Begin in Bridge of Earn, just off junction 9 on the M90. Leave Bridge of Earn on the B935, heading west. Continue west along the B935, through Forgandenny. Forgandenny was once the ancient Pictish capital of the land that was to become Scotland. After Forgandenny, turn left up a quiet lane through a wood, signed 'Path of Condie'. Ignore the first right turn after a mile, but take the second right 600 metres after this, where the road starts to climb steeply. Cross the Water of May and climb steadily.

Once you get to the top of the hill, you should bear right, shortly after the farm: Mains of Condie. Do not descend to Path of Condie. The descent to Dunning begins gently but becomes steep – so check your brakes! Dunning is a quiet village with a long history. It's dominated by St Serf's Church (1219), with its impressive Norman tower dating from the mid-twelfth century. The Pictish Dupplin Cross can be seen inside (entry is free).

Leave Dunning on the B8062, heading west. A mile beyond the village, turn right to a minor road. Just before this, you pass a monument to Maggie Wells, who was burned as a witch in 1657 (+ on map). Cross the railway. Look across the A9 main road and you will see a gate on the opposite side. Taking care, cross over the main road and go through the gate to enter Aberuthven. Turn left on to the A824 to go through the village. Immediately after crossing a river, turn right to a minor road leading to Kinkell Bridge.

This minor road rises at first, giving views towards the northern hills, then there is a drop to the B8062 leading to Kinkell Bridge. Turn right here, then turn right again to cross the bridge. After the bridge, turn right again, heading towards Trinity Gask. Immediately after this, turn left for Kirkton. You pass a church, then the road winds up Chapelhill, then drops to Dubheads, where you turn right. Turn right again at the next junction. You can identify this by the presence of a contractor who builds garden sheds.

The road climbs again. Go over the line of the Roman road at Findo Gask, then descend steeply to the A9. Take care crossing, and continue on to Dunning. After this, use the minor road which skirts the northern edge of the Ochils. This is fairly quiet and very pretty. Access to this from Dunning is from near the village shop. Halfway back to Bridge of Earn, you meet the B935 again. Continue in the same direction, going east through Forgandenny to Bridge of Earn.

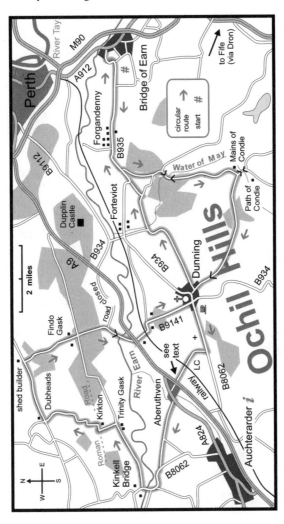

LOCH AN EILEAN TO GLEN FESHIE

A circular in Caledonian pine woods
Route grading: **Easy – mountain bike** (24 miles)

This circular route is really a figure of eight. Each loop is 12 miles so you could do these separately or combine them for a 24-mile route. The part round Loch an Eilean is a popular walk. Thank walkers, if they give way. You might prefer to walk the footpath sections.

Northern loop – Access to Loch an Eilean is from the B970, running from Inverdruie to Feshiebridge. Cross the river where it flows out of the loch, then bear right following the loch shore. After a mile, you come to a fork in the track. Bear right to continue round the loch.

The path on this next section is less wide, so watch out for pedestrians. You have to leave the trail round Loch an Eilean and cut south to Loch Gamhna. This isn't signposted. It's a left turn 100 metres after crossing a small burn: a narrow footpath. Once you get to Loch Gamhna, you have to take another left turn otherwise you'll end up going right round Loch Gamhna and back to Loch an Eilean. Turn left at the first junction. After two miles, you pass a small bothy (rough shelter) and will see the trees of a plantation forest ahead. Enter the forest.

The path becomes a forest road. Bear left at a marker post and continue straight on for a mile. Take the second left at four ways junction for Feshiebridge. You reach the public road by some wooden chalets or huts. Turn left here, if you are doing the southern loop up Glen Feshie, otherwise turn right. Turn right at the B970 to return to Loch an Eilean. The road runs through trees for just over four miles, passing a plant nursery at Inshriach. Finally, you see a sign for Loch an Eilean – your starting point is up this road.

Southern loop – Start from the junction of the B970 and the Glen Feshie road, leading to Lagganlia just north of Feshiebridge. Go south on the minor road that leads to Achlean. The road ends at Achlean. Two rough paths lead off from here. One goes up the hill to the mountain Carn Bàn Mór. We are taking the other path, which goes up the glen near the river, where you might prefer to walk for a mile.

Pass between a small hill and a cottage. Cross a burn, then a flat area with grass and heather. Pass a ruined cottage, then cross the bridge to the road and turn right down the glen. After four miles, you pass Uath Lochan – a pretty spot. After this, the road descends and you turn right on to the B970. The next junction is a minor road, leading to Kincraig. Keep straight on. There's a gentle climb then a dip at Feshiebridge, the river tumbling through a narrow gorge. Keep straight on to return to the start.

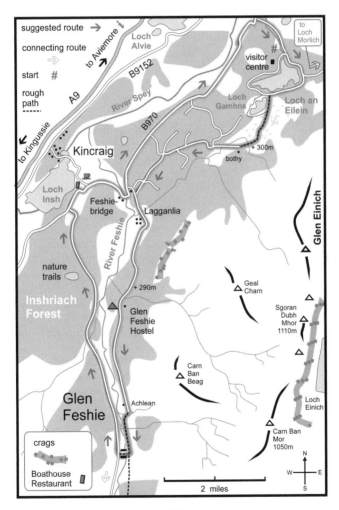

SPEY BAY TO CRAIGELLACHIE

An interesting ride, partly on the Speyside Way
Route grading: **Varied – mountain bike** (18 miles)

The Speyside Way runs from Spey Bay to Aviemore. Bikes are allowed on much of it as far as Ballindalloch. South of this, you can continue to Aviemore using minor-road alternatives (see following pages). The National Cycle Network Route 1 also runs through Spey Bay.

The Speyside Way starts near the Tugnet Ice House at Spey Bay (café). Another way to get to the start is via Garmouth, using the Spey Viaduct Walk. Join it by picnic tables as you enter Garmouth on the B9105.

You should cycle on the B9104, as cycling is not allowed on the river footpath. These merge just before you enter Fochabers. Enter the town by turning left on the main road, and avoid the traffic by using the marked cyclepaths. Fochabers is an attractive small town. Leave the town by continuing east along the main street (A96), then turn right (south) just before a school. Do not continue to the A98/A96 junction.

At Boat o' Brig cross the B9103 – this can be busy. Turn right, then immediately left up steps by a house with a portico to leave the public road. Follow Speyside Way signs, climbing then turning left at farm buildings. Follow an electricity line into the forest. Turn right uphill again at a gun club sign.

The track dips into Ben Aigan Forest, then skirts it, giving good views of the Spey valley. After this, it enters the forest, and climbs steeply to a forest road. Turn right here. There is an initial drop, a further climb, then turn right at the forest road junctions. Finally, there is a fast descent to leave the forest at a mountain biking sign.

Turn left onto the public road and descend further. Turn right at the A95 to enter Craigellachie. You can camp here (cold water only). Craigellachie has a Spar food shop. There is a pub with a riverside garden, hotels and a choice of B&Bs.

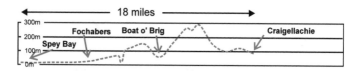

SPEY BAY TO CRAIGELLACHIE

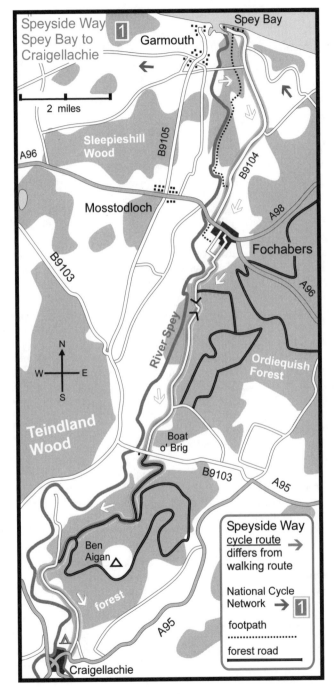

Speyside Way
Spey Bay to
Craigellachie

1

Garmouth

Spey Bay

2 miles

Sleepieshill
Wood

B9105

A96

B9104

A98

Mosstodloch

Fochabers

B9103

A96

River Spey

N
W   E
S

Ordiequish
Forest

Teindland
Wood

Boat
o' Brig

B9103

A95

Ben
Aigan
△

forest

Speyside Way
<u>cycle route</u> →
differs from
walking route

National Cycle
Network → 1

footpath
....

forest road
━━━━━━

A95

△
Craigellachie

109

CRAIGELLACHIE TO BALLINDALLOCH

The Speyside Way part is on a former railway line
Route grading: **Easy (return leg Hilly) – any bike** (24 miles)

The outward part of this route is entirely on the former Strathspey railway line, so the gradients are very easy. The railway follows the river, so the views are pretty good too. The route is studded with famous distilleries, all producing the smooth Speyside malt whisky. The dirt surface of the railway path is generally quite smooth. South of Craigellachie, there are some grassy sections.

In Craigellachie, by the Speyside Way ranger's office, turn right onto the old railway line (turning left takes you to Dufftown). The track bed runs under the main road, then follows the river bank. There is a small tunnel. The route runs through a park in Aberlour. There is a tearoom in the old station building run by ladies from the local church. An alternative would be the Station Bar.

After this, the route rolls along by the river through mixed woodland. You pass the former halt of Dailuaine, cross a minor road, then cross the river on a combined road and rail bridge (the 'rail' part of which is now a cyclepath). Turn left onto the path again. The track runs by the Knockando and Tamdhu distilleries.

After Tamdhu, the path runs high above the river, giving lovely views. Cross the small viaduct and take the steps down. You pass under the B9102 at Blacksboat, where there are picnic tables, then you roll along by wide meanders in the river to the former railway bridge at Ballindalloch. Cross the bridge to Ballindalloch station.

Returning to Craigellachie by road, the distance is the same but there are hills. Cross back over the River Spey, using the old railway bridge, then join the B9102 using an access road. Turn right onto the B9102. You might also like to note that you can get to Grantown-on-Spey by turning left at this point (see following page).

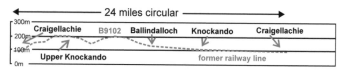

Dufftown Spur is 4 miles away. Follow the old Strathspey railway line from Craigellachie to Dufftown, up the valley of the River Fiddich. To reach the Spur from Craigellachie, turn left from the Speyside Way ranger's office and follow the path past the toilet block.

The route ends in Balvenie, at a picnic area just outside the town, by the Glenfiddich distillery. Balvenie Castle, the impressive thirteenth-century lair of John Comyn (who was known as the Black Comyn and died in 1300), is next to the distillery. This is a large castle building. It was a noble residence for 400 years and was visited by Edward the First in 1304 and by Mary Queen of Scots in 1562. There is also a museum in Dufftown, with displays of local history. Also worth visiting is Mortlach Church, which has been in continual use for public worship since 566.

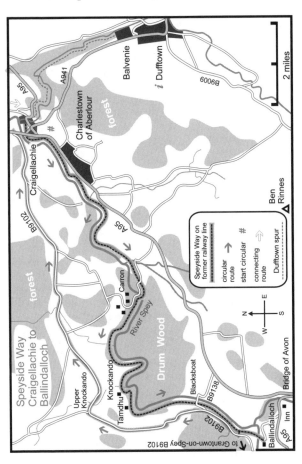

BALLINDALLOCH TO AVIEMORE

It is not possible to cycle the central part of the Speyside
Way – take this route instead
Route grading: **Varied** (28 miles)

Between Ballindalloch and Grantown-on-Spey, the Speyside
way is a walking route only. You can bypass this section by
using the B9102. This is a beautiful hilly ride by the north
bank of the River Spey. At the south end of this, you arrive at
the A939 and Grantown-on-Spey. This is a traditional
Highland town, with a tourist information centre, shops,
hotels, etc.

To continue to Aviemore, keep on the A939, turning left at
the traffic lights, then straight on at a roundabout to cross the
River Spey. A little way after crossing, the river turns right to
the B970 at a sign for Nethy Bridge. At this point, if you look
to your right, you will see the Speyside Way again. It runs
along an old railway line, and the surface is quite good for
cycling. The only snag is that there are quite a lot of gates to
open and shut. If you think you might find this a bit tedious,
keep on the B970. You arrive in Nethy Bridge, whichever way
you go.

Nethy Bridge, though smaller than Grantown-on-Spey, has
a hotel doing bar food, a shop and a tearoom. Leave the
village, travelling south on the B970 but take a left turn to a
minor road immediately south of the village. The Speyside
Way goes this way also but it leaves the road after a while,
following a line of pylons. Ignore this, keeping straight on into
Abernethy Forest. Bear right at the next two junctions,
following signs for Loch Garten.

Loch Garten is very pretty. It is a nature reserve and the
place where ospreys were reintroduced to the Highlands.
There is a hide and an RSPB web camera showing the nesting
site.

After passing the loch, you meet the B970 again. Turn left
here, then right to cross over the River Spey to Boat of

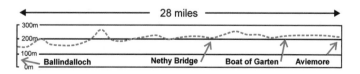

112

Garten. Between Boat of Garten and Aviemore, you simply follow the railway line again, which is a combined Speyside Way/National Cycle Network route. A steam tourist train runs beside the cycle route in summer. Following this route will take you into the centre of Aviemore.

Aviemore has most things, including a youth hostel, tourist information, ski shops, supermarkets, Burger King, swimming pool, ice rink, but architecturally it's not particularly attractive. They are supposed to be doing something about that. There's a good youth hostel and forest campsite five miles away, up the ski road at Glenmore.

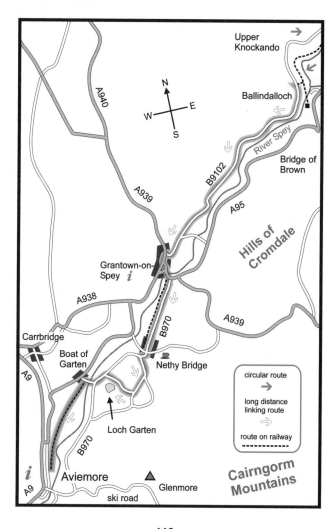

ABERNETHY FOREST AND THE PASS OF RYVOAN

Forest roads and paths with some public road – great views!
Route grading: **Varied – mountain bike** (21 miles)

It would be possible to cycle this route on any bike. Inexperienced riders, or those not using mountain bikes, would have to walk in a few places.

This description is circular, starting from Nethy Bridge. There is a tearoom and a hotel doing bar lunches at Nethy Bridge and a café in the shop at Glenmore. Abernethy Forest, like Rothiemurchus further south, is a remnant of the native Scots pine forest that once covered the Highlands. This forest is the habitat of red squirrels, wildcats, pine martens and red deer. Ospreys were re-established near Loch Garten in the 1950s.

In Nethy Bridge, take the minor road between the post office and the River Nethy, travelling west. This climbs gently, then turns south to the forest, becoming a track. Keep straight on, ignoring any left turns, until you come to a T junction and can go no further. Turn left here to travel east, then take the second turning to the right (100 metres before the forest lodge).

There is a fork in the track near here. Of the two trails, the right-hand one (not highlighted on the map) is the more difficult. Both paths climb steadily, becoming narrower.

When you leave the trees, most of the climbing is done. Cairngorm Mountain will be visible ahead. The path becomes rocky and more Scots pine appear. Then, after reaching open country again, you pass Ryvoan Bothy (rough shelter). Usually there will be someone camping there.

Shortly after this, there is a rocky descent; many people might prefer to walk here. The path enters Glenmore Forest Park. Despite being sandy in places, it is quite fast (be

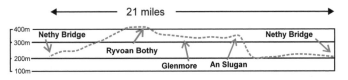

considerate to walkers) and mainly downhill.

Soon you pass Lochan Uaine, with its steep crags above, and then drop to a small bridge. After this, at Glenmore Lodge, the track finally becomes a road. Reward yourself with an apple strudel at the Glenmore shop tearoom; this is beside Glenmore Campsite.

Cycle west from Glenmore, passing along the north side of Loch Morlich. You can either use the public road to do this or follow a track by the loch shore. Just before the end of the loch, turn right into the Queen's Forest. Remain on this forest road for four miles, ignoring all left and right turns. You will eventually come out on the B970, where you turn right.

You should be on the B970 for only one mile, after which you turn right again to a very narrow minor road. This takes you through Abernethy Forest, passing quite near to Loch Garten, then eventually back to Nethy Bridge.

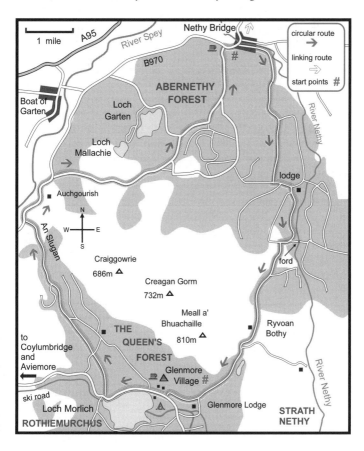

AROUND LOCH NESS

Quiet routes near a famous loch
Route grading: **Hilly** (80 miles, or shorter options
– Loch Ness circular)

If you are cycling anywhere near Loch Ness, try to avoid the
A82. This road is narrow in places and it carries heavy traffic.

The minor roads to the south-east of Loch Ness are quite
quiet and very pretty. The B852 runs along the shore of the
loch, giving excellent views. The other roads, by Lochs Ashie,
Duntelchaig, Ruthven and Mhór, are steep in places, but the
suggested circular on the map keeps at high level most of the
time. The main climb is out of Inverness. There is a long
descent to the shore of Loch Ness for the return leg but there
are no serious hills after that.

Eating places on the south-east side of Loch Ness are a pub
at Dores; a tearoom at Foyers; the Whitebridge Hotel; a herb
nursery, and the Grouse and Trout Hotel, both on the B851.

The other option suggested on the map is a circuit right
round Loch Ness. This would take two days. The route takes
advantage of forest roads on the north side of Loch Ness. These
are signposted as the 'Great Glen Cycle Route'. Between Fort
Augustus and Drumnadrochit, it is mostly forest roads
(mountain biking). North of this, the route is on public roads.

From Fort Augustus, go north on the A82 for 1.5 miles to a
picnic site. Turn left into the forest, following the signs. It's seven
miles on hilly forest trails to Invermoriston. There is a long
sweep round to the west to make the descent to Invermoriston,
then a steep drop to a T junction, where you turn right.

At Invermoriston, you enter forest again behind the
Glenmoriston Arms Hotel. This section is more arduous but

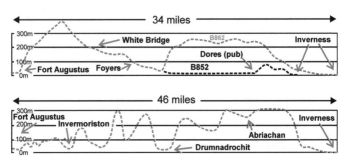

has good views. You climb steeply at first on a surfaced road. After four miles, this ends near Loch Ness Youth Hostel. The next part is a stiff climb of 300m, a high-level section, then a link to join a minor road leading to Drumnadrochit. The minor road emerges on to the A82 by the River Coiltie.

In Drumnadrochit, turn left onto the A831 for 1.5 miles, then right onto the A833 (signed 'Beauly') to climb out of Glen Urquhart. After five miles, turn right for Abriachan (signed 'Foxhole'). Bear right at the next two junctions (signed 'Drumnadrochit via Loch Ness'). Just before Abriachan, turn left at a crossroads (signed 'Blackfold'), passing a phone box. Drop steeply to the A82 for Inverness. In Inverness, cross the canal bridge and turn east to Bught Lane and follow the river to the town centre.

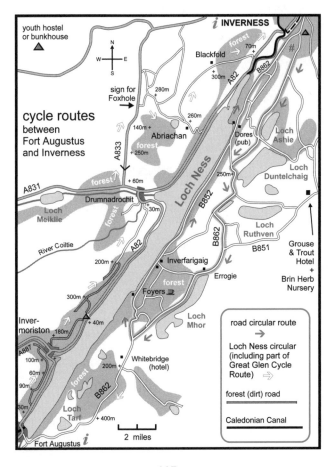

NORTHERN HIGHLANDS

DISTANCES AND ROUTE GRADING

CHAPTER 5

NORTHERN HIGHLANDS

The area covered in this chapter is mainland Scotland, north of the Great Glen. The northern Highlands contain some of the wildest and most beautiful scenery in Scotland. Because of the nature of the terrain, there are fewer roads.

The scenery in the west is dramatic but the roads are hilly. Quiet circular routes are difficult to find. There are, however, a number of really beautiful minor roads running up quiet glens, and this chapter aims to highlight them.

In addition to the day rides, there is a long distance route in the far north-west of Scotland. This is a circular route that would take a week. Sections of it would make excellent day rides and some could be made circular.

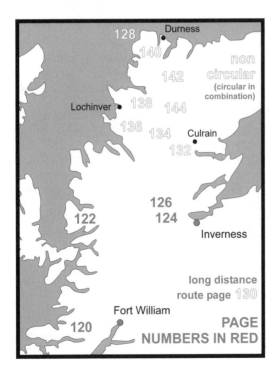

ARDGOUR AND LOCH SHIEL

Challenging, wonderful scenery
Route grading: **Hilly – mountain bike** (59 miles)

This route is on a rough track for 13 miles, and the rest of it is on public roads. There are views of lochs and mountains all the way. To get round in a day, you need to be fit and not dally too long over breakfast! To take it more easily, give yourself two days. There is overnight accommodation in Glenfinnan, Corran and Strontian. The scenery certainly justifies lingering. The description starts from Glenfinnan.

Glenfinnan is the place where Bonnie Prince Charlie first rallied the clans in his attempt to install the Stuart dynasty to the British throne. The site is marked by the Glenfinnan monument. The route starts just over a mile east of this, at a bridge carrying a dirt road over the River Callop. A bridge carrying the railway over the A830 is 500 metres further east. Go east under the railway bridge, then turn right to the south side of Loch Eil along the A861 (passing places).

By Loch Eil and Loch Linnhe, it's mostly flat. The scenery becomes more dramatic as you turn the corner and see the cliffs of Ben Nevis (1344m). A foot passenger ferry runs across Loch Linnhe to Fort William (not Sundays). This takes bikes. It could be a place to start, if you are staying in Fort William.

The road gives regular views of Loch Linnhe. Most traffic is carried on the A82 on the other side of the loch. There is a hotel at Corran serving food. South of Corran, the road ceases to be single track. Cars crossing over on the ferry are going to Mull or Ardnamurchan. They will pass in groups of perhaps eight cars at twenty-minute intervals. The road should be fairly quiet apart from this.

As you enter Strontian, there is a little shop that sells ice cream, etc. There's a larger supermarket in the village and a choice of hotels, B&Bs, etc. Strontian gives its name to the element strontium, which was discovered here.

Continue through Strontian village until you cross Strontian River, then turn right. After this, avoid all turn-offs. Eventually the road becomes so steep that you wonder why anyone bothered to build it (it was, in fact, built to extract strontianite). The descent is also steep. At the bottom, turn left to cross over the river then left again after the bridge.

Keep going on the forest road. There's a climb, then a descent to Loch Shiel. The track winds along by the shore much of the time. Take your time and enjoy the views over the loch towards the mountains of Moidart. There is another route in this area in The Western Islands chapter of this book (page 158).

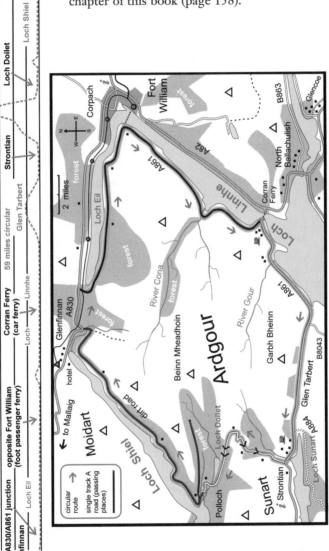

121

APPLECROSS AND LOCH TORRIDON

Challenging, wonderful scenery
Route grading: **Hilly** (45 miles)

The Applecross Peninsula is opposite the islands of Raasay and Skye. The Bealach na Ba, or Pass of the Cattle, is an old drove road used in past times to take cattle to the market. The public road was completed in 1975. Prior to this, the coast was only accessible on foot or by sea.

The Bealach na Ba is the highest road pass in Scotland, at 626m above sea level. It is too steep to freewheel down on its south side and has many hairpin bends. Cycling northward, there is more of a cruising descent to Applecross.

The views of the Applecross hills, the Cuillin of Skye and the bay are superb. Further north, there are views of the Torridon Mountains and Loch Torridon. As the route approaches Shieldaig (mile off-route), there are frequent steep, short hills. There is a café by Shieldaig on the A896.

The Applecross Inn has local seafood, and the Flower Tunnel in Applecross and Tigh a'Crachaich near Kenmore on the north coast road do snacks and beverages. The Inn has accommodation and there is self-catering accommodation and B&Bs nearby. There's a campsite at Applecross. There is a bakery at the Flower Tunnel, and also a food shop in Applecross with groceries and spirits, etc.

There are a number of other local roads nearby which make interesting cycling. The coast road leading west from Lochcarron leads to ruined Strome Castle at Stromeferry. In 1602, a siege of the castle ended abruptly when the cooks made the fatal mistake of putting water in the gunpowder. Despite the name, there is no ferry at Stromeferry. The road continues beyond the castle and has fine views.

The area around the famously scenic village of Plockton is

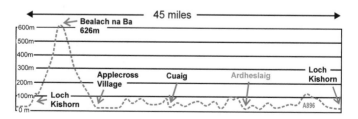

interesting to explore on a bike. It might be busy in summer and there are many blind corners, so it needs care. You could make use of the Kyle of Lochalsh line for combined cycle/train rides.

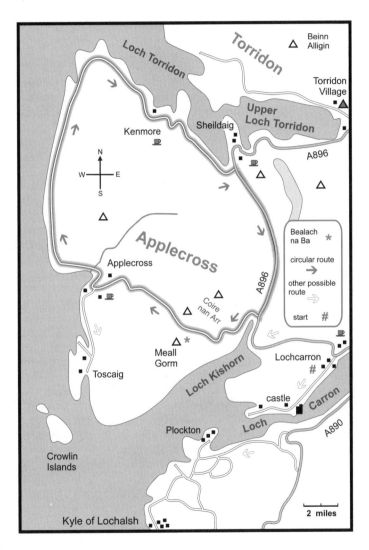

RIVER BEAULY AND STRATHFARRAR

A wonderful quiet glen with native pine forests, a convenient inn halfway
Route grading: **Varied** (48 miles)

As you will see from the map, this route has two parts. You could do one of these only for a shorter option. Begin in the village of Beauly, which is ten miles west of Inverness. In Beauly, travel south on the A862 for a short distance, then turn right onto the A831. After a mile, turn left to a minor road which crosses over the River Beauly. Immediately after the bridge, turn right by a line of pylons, signed 'Fanellan'.

After a short climb and a brief descent, the road follows the south bank of the river for five miles. After this, take a right fork, crossing the river again to Struy. This turn-off is just after Erchless Castle, which you will see on the far river bank.

After crossing the river, turn right on to the A831 for a very short distance, then turn left off the main road by the River Farrar. The Inn at Struy can provide tea, coffee, meals, etc.

The road up Strathfarrar has a gate. The gate is sometimes unlocked. The estate has special arrangements to allow hillwalkers' cars through at certain times. None of this is a problem for a bicycle – just go round the barrier.

The road here is mainly for the hydro-power station further up. It gives access to some lovely scenery, with natural woods of Scots pine, backed by mountains rising to over 1,000 metres. The river tumbles over many waterfalls, and there are many picnic spots on the way which take advantage of this.

There are some fairly steep short hills initially but once you have reached Loch Beannacharan most of the climbing is over. There is a stiff final ascent to the dam at Loch Monar. Most people seem to prefer to return to Beauly on the A831. This should not be a problem, as it is fairly quiet.

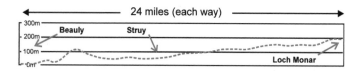

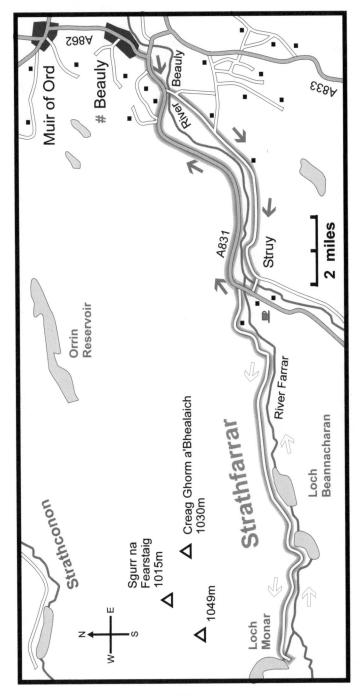

LOCH ACHILTY AND STRATHCONON

This quiet glen is up and back – wonderful in both directions!
Route grading: **Easy** (38 miles)

This is one of the loveliest glens in Scotland and usually very quiet. You have to go up and down again but it is so pretty, it is twice the pleasure. This is an area that is sheltered from western winds. The scenery is definitely Highland but it rains less here than it does further west.

In Contin, take a minor road leading west. This starts from near the Achilty Hotel (food, coffee, etc.). The road passes by the shore of Loch Achilty, then after four miles you meet a little bridge over the River Conon. Turn left over this, then after a further mile, cycle over the dam at the head of Loch Meig. After the dam, turn right up the glen.

The road climbs gently up the glen on the south side of the River Meig, then crosses over to the north side at Bridgend. After this, the glen becomes steep-sided, though the road remains quite gentle. There are many attractive picnic spots by the river. The road ends at Loch Beannacharain.

Return down the glen the way you came. Do not cross the Loch Meig dam but continue on down the glen, following the south bank of the River Meig, then the River Conon.

When you come to Loch Achonachie and see the power station, cross over the Loch Achonachie dam by turning sharp left off the public road. After this, follow a fairly rough farm track across a field for two miles to return to Contin.

If cycling along the farm track does not appeal, you can of course return to Contin the way you came. The alternative is the A832/A835, crossing the river further east. The A835 has fast traffic. The minor road to Muir of Ord is quite pretty.

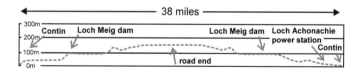

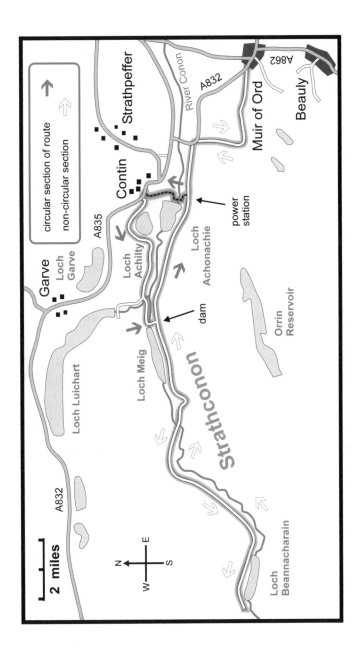

KYLE OF DURNESS TO CAPE WRATH

A journey to the north-west tip of Scotland
Route grading: **Hilly – any bike** (22 miles)

The route to Cape Wrath was at one time a surfaced road, but it's in poor condition now. Perhaps it's cheaper nowadays to supply the lighthouse by helicopter than maintain the road. The track to Cape Wrath is separated from the rest of the road network by the Kyle of Durness. A foot passenger ferry takes you over. The only other vehicle on the road will be a minibus that operates a shuttle service. The minibus is taken over by a lighter at the start and end of the tourist season.

Bear in mind that there's no shelter of any kind along the way, so the route is very exposed. The ferry service is frequent in summer, but because the Kyle of Durness is tidal, the ferry can only operate at certain times – phone 01971 511376. The hotel by the ferry provides teas.

As soon as you get off the ferry, there's a climb. There's a great view over the Kyle of Durness towards Balnakeil. Following this, you plunge to sea level again to cross a little bridge over the Daill River, before turning west away from the sea. After a while, you pass quite close to the conical hill of Maovally and the crags of Fashven are clearly visible to the south. Shortly after this, another track runs down to an attractive beach at Kearvaig. There is an interesting rock stack here, Clo Kearvaig (Cathedral Rock).

On the main route, there's a gradual descent to cross the Kearvaig River. After that, the remaining four miles to the lighthouse are not too difficult. Once you get to Cape Wrath, if you look east, you should be able to see the high cliffs at Clo Mor, as well as the rock stack Clo Kearvaig. If it's windy, you'll have had a tough journey, but the surf on the rocks below will be impressive. The return journey to the Kyle of Durness should be much quicker. You did remember to check on the return ferry times, didn't you?

Cape Wrath is not the most northerly point in mainland

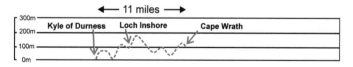

KYLE OF DURNESS TO CAPE WRATH

Scotland. That distinction belongs to Dunnett Head. The highest sea cliffs in mainland Britain are here, however, 920 feet high at nearby Clo Mor. The lighthouse at Cape Wrath was completed in 1828. The engineer was Robert Stevenson, grandfather of the author Robert Louis Stevenson. Until quite recently, this was a manned lighthouse. Cape Wrath was one of the last to be made fully automatic.

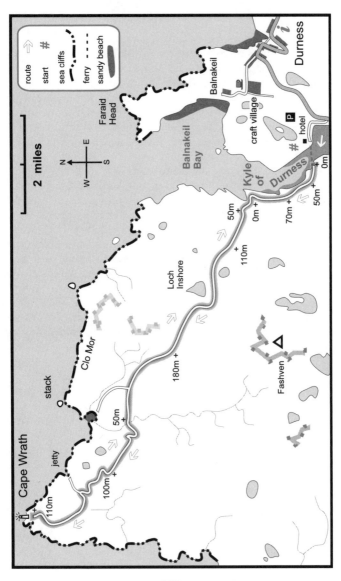

THE FAR NORTH-WEST

A long distance route in some of the wildest and most rugged scenery in Scotland
Route grading: **Hilly** (190 miles)

See following pages for detailed description. If you like road cycling and hills to get your teeth into, this area is for you!

The far north-west contains some of the wildest and most beautiful scenery in Scotland, but there aren't very many roads. Despite this, traffic is likely to be reasonably light. Many car drivers who come as far north as Ullapool will be catching the ferry to Stornoway on the island of Lewis. The roads are mostly hilly. In fact, some roads hardly have a flat yard on them.

Getting to the start: the route starts from Culrain, which is a train station on the North Highland Railway Line. This is quite a short train journey north from Inverness. Scotrail make special arrangements in the summer to let people travel with bicycles. Most long distance rail travellers will be coming from further south, however, so it's important to check that there will be space for your bike on every leg of your train journey. You may want to use Carbisdale Castle Youth Hostel as an overnight stop, as it's near Culrain train station. There is also a choice of hotels and B&Bs in the area, particularly around Bonar Bridge and Lairg. (Culrain can also be a useful starting point for the ferry from Ullapool to Stornoway on Lewis.)

There are B&Bs in most of the population centres, and quite a number of hotels, many of them catering for fishermen. The Youth Hostel network is still mostly intact and there are independent hostels. There aren't a lot of back roads, but those that do exist are particularly beautiful, so allow time to explore.

This is quite a hilly area, with some long climbs. In Assynt, the hills are steep but the beaches are lovely and the mountains are quite unlike any others. North of Assynt, the hills are better-graded but often longer. The fishing port of Kinlochbervie is interesting and you can walk, or possibly mountain bike, to beautiful Sandwood Bay.

Further north again, it's possible to cycle to Cape Wrath, the furthest point of Scotland's north-west seaboard. John o' Groats is slightly further north but Cape Wrath is much more impressive.

Durness has sandy beaches, interesting caves and a craft village. The road south from Durness, via Ben Hope and Ben Klibreck, is again a place of wide open spaces and few people.

One thing that you will often meet on this route is single track roads with passing places. The single track carriageway is often wide enough to let a car and a bike pass each other without stopping. Travelling in this area on a bike will certainly leave you with the feeling that not everywhere on this planet is a crowded place.

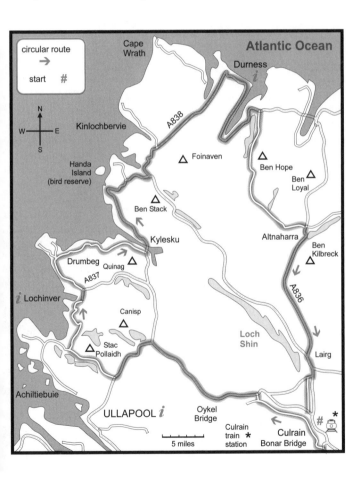

CULRAIN TO LEDMORE JUNCTION

A gentle climb into wonderful scenery
Route grading: **Varied** (27 miles)

As mentioned on page 130, you can get a train to Culrain, but it's also possible to cycle from Inverness using the National Cycle Network. Route 1 goes via the Black Isle and is also part of the wider international North Sea Cycle Route.

Culrain might be wee but there are two train stations, Culrain and Invershin, the other side of the Kyle of Sutherland. In the past, there wasn't any way for people to get over the kyle other than on the train, hence the need for two stations. Flag the train down, incidentally.

Once there were dire warnings in Carbisdale Castle Youth Hostel, telling cyclists not to use the rail bridge. Using this bridge saved you an eight-mile diversion via Bonar Bridge going north, so not a few risked the wrath of British Rail and sneaked over. There is now a footbridge, so it's certainly not worth risking your life just to avoid a few steps.

Carbisdale Castle was built as part of the divorce settlement of the Duchess of Sutherland, so it's not really very old. During the Second World War, the King of Norway lived there. Whether you are staying there or in a B&B, it's important to begin the route on the west side of the Kyle of Sutherland. Coming north from Inverness, you turn left at Ardgay before crossing the bridge over the Kyle to Bonar Bridge. This first section of the route will be signed with 'Route 1' cycle signs.

Our route and the National Route go different ways near Culrain station. The National Route crosses over the Kyle to the A836 using a footbridge, while we continue north, then west, on the minor road on the west side of the Kyle.

This lovely little minor road runs through wooded scenery for nine miles. The Kyle of Sutherland is on the right but this eventually narrows and becomes the River Oykel. Turn right

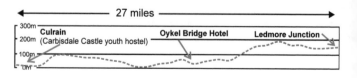

27 miles

300m
200m
100m
0m

Culrain
(Carbisdale Castle youth hostel)

Oykel Bridge Hotel

Ledmore Junction

to cross the river at the sign for Rosehall and Oykel Bridge. Turn left onto the A837.

After five miles, you cross the river again at Oykel Bridge (hotel). The road begins a steady climb, with the river on the right-hand side. After two miles, the road leaves the river, climbing more steeply for three miles towards Loch Craggie. From this point, you get distant views of the magic mountains of Assynt.

Most obvious of these is Suilven, which rises steeply from a glacier-scored plateau. By now the road is narrow, with passing places. It runs through forest at times, but at Loch Borralan it opens out again and you get closer views of the hills. Turn left at Ledmore Junction, signed 'Ullapool'. There is a tearoom three miles further west on the A835 at Elphin.

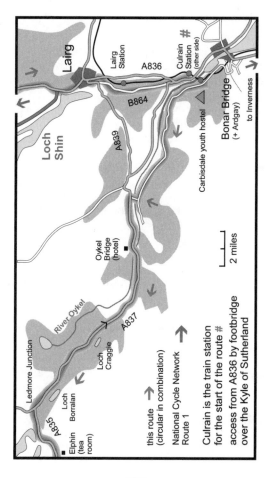

LEDMORE JUNCTION TO STAC POLLAIDH

Some of the most interesting scenery in Scotland
Route grading: **Varied** (17 miles)

Stac Pollaidh is a very much eroded but still much loved
Scottish mountain. I took a group of Americans here a few
years ago. They were experienced cyclists, who had ridden
widely in the USA, Canada and Europe. At the end, they said
it had been the best bike ride ever. Fortunately, the weather
had been kind. There are often long spells of settled weather
in the early summer.

The area falls into two parts, as far as cycling is concerned:
Coigach, to the south, is not dreadfully hilly. Cycling this is
inevitably out and back. A rough track is shown on some maps,
leading from the end of the road east of Achiltiebuie to the
A835 near Strath Kanaird. This is difficult scrambling and
taking a bike is out of the question.

All the same, you should go to Altandhu, Achiltiebuie, etc.
There are some lovely beaches, combined with distant views
of the mountains to the north. There are also interesting
places to visit.

Further north, in Assynt, it's fairly hilly. A B&B owner in
Lochinver once told me that she was expecting a family from
Surrey one evening. They planned to cycle from Kylesku via
Drumbeg. They knew it was hilly but it was only 25 miles after
all. She got a phone call at 3 p.m. in the afternoon, and they
weren't even halfway round – she drove round and collected
them.

As mentioned earlier, there is a tearoom at Elphin. There is
also a Farm Centre, which has over 36 rare breeds of farm
animals, ancient and modern. This is a working croft adapted
for education, conservation and organic farming. It has a
tearoom too. There's a Scottish jewellery/lapidary centre just
south of this.

The A835 here is the main road to the north-west, so
depending on the time of day there is certain to be some traffic

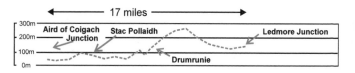

on it. The road is reasonably wide and the sight lines are mostly good but there are some tight bends around Elphin. You will be on it for eight miles, after which you turn right into Inverpolly for Achiltiebuie, Lochinver, etc.

There's an initial climb, then you drop down to Loch Lurgainn. This has sandy beaches and a number of islets covered in trees – once all the Highlands were like this. A noticeboard opposite Stac Pollaidh gives information about the nature reserve; the mountain is a popular climb. Shortly after Stac Pollaidh, you reach the road junction at Aird of Coigach, where you have to make a decision.

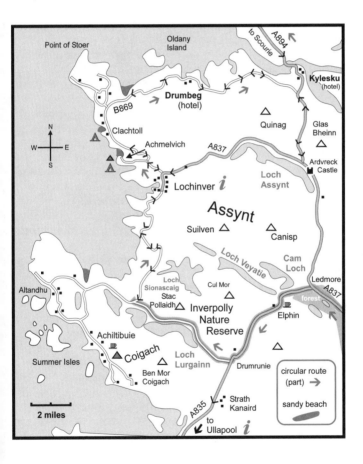

STAC POLLAIDH TO ACHILTIEBUIE

Some of the most interesting scenery in Scotland
Route grading: **Varied** (12 miles)

Cycling to Achiltibuie, you should go the longer way via
Altandhu. There is a wonderful panorama of the Summer
Isles a mile before Altandhu, making the extra distance well
worthwhile. There's a pub called the Fuaran Bar at
Altandhu. Also there's a fish smokehouse, where you can see
fish being smoked and, of course, buy the product.

Just south of Altandhu is Old Dornie harbour, opposite Isle
Ristol, a pleasant place to stop. Further on, you'll pass a craft
and coffee shop at Polbain. Continuing south again, you run
into Achiltiebuie.

Achiltiebuie has the Hydroponicum, a warm damp place to sit
if it's cold and damp outside. This is a complex of greenhouses,
with plants grown without soil. You can have a guided tour or
simply sit and drink coffee surrounded by all the flowers.

The population around here is concentrated in small
crofting communities. The majority of these lie along the
rocky coastline, either to the north or south of the village
and at the fishing port of Lochinver. Inchnadamph, situated
on the shores of Loch Assynt, and its southerly neighbour
of Elphin, are also areas of inland settlement.

The geology of this area is quite unusual so it's worth saying
a little about it. The main rocks are of the Cambrian period,
including an extremely hard and shiny quartzite, which makes
for a barren countryside. Here and there, however, there are
outcrops of limestone. In these areas, instead of bareness and
peat, there is the sudden appearance of greenness and rich soil.
It's no surprise that these are the areas of settlement in Assynt.

As far as wildlife goes, the many lochs support black- and
red-throated divers, and waders including redshank, curlew
and greenshank. Oystercatchers can be seen along the coast or
by the loch shores.

Numerous birds are found inland on the moors, including

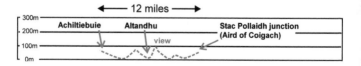

stonechats, wheatears and meadow pipits. Inchnadamph has a colony of swallows and house martins – the only ones in Assynt. Birds of prey include the buzzard, peregrine falcon, kestrel and marlin. The golden eagle is occasionally seen in the more remote and undisturbed areas.

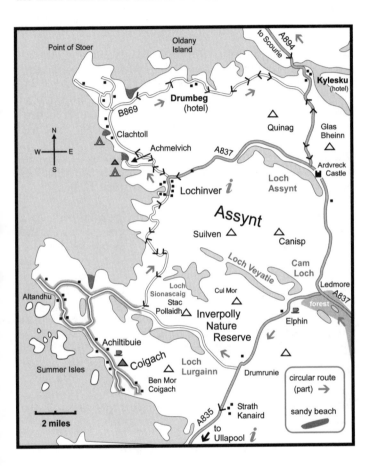

STAC POLLAIDH, LOCHINVER AND KYLESKU

Possibly the most scenic road in Scotland
Route grading: **Hilly** (38 miles)

Possibly the most scenic road in Scotland, and certainly the most hilly! You should allow plenty of time for cycling between the Stac Pollaidh junction and Lochinver.

There are occasional views of the mountains and the road drops steeply to some lovely bays. There are a lot of lochans with water lilies. South of Lochinver, you cross the River Kirkaig, which is the start of the walking route to Suilven.

Lochinver is an important fishing centre. It also has the Culag Hotel, a good supermarket, a post office and a number of other shops. The youth hostel is four miles further on, at Achmelvich.

If you are a mountain biker, you might be tempted to try a footpath shown on OS maps running between Suilven and Canisp. This is not a good idea. The access point has a sign: 'no bikes please', and in any case, if you try it, you'll be carrying your bike, not riding it.

The route from Lochinver to Kylesku goes via Drumbeg. In days gone by, you could camp wild on the coast here but erosion problems have meant that campers are concentrated at two sites, Achmelvich and Clachtoll. The start of the road is signed 'Kylesku Tourist Route'.

There are a number of minor roads leading towards the Point of Stoer, which are worth exploring. Just before Stoer, you come to a memorial to the Rev Norman MacLeod, who eventually settled in New Zealand with his followers. On the way, they also tried Nova Scotia and Australia – all by sailing ship too.

After Stoer, you pass the golden sand of Clashnessie Bay, then climb up to Drumbeg, where there is a hotel. After this, there is another plunge to Loch Nedd – watch out for sharp bends. There is a sign saying '25% descent'. Is it possible to have a road with 25% descent? It certainly it seems like it.

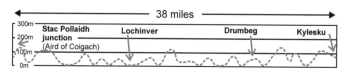

Towards the end, you get the occasional dramatic view of the mountain Quinag. The road joins the A894 just south of Kylesku. There is a hotel at Kylesku doing bar food. You can also take a boat to the Eas Coul Aulin Falls, the tallest waterfall in Britain, a 200-metre drop. This is not a big waterfall in volume but the surrounding scenery is undeniably impressive.

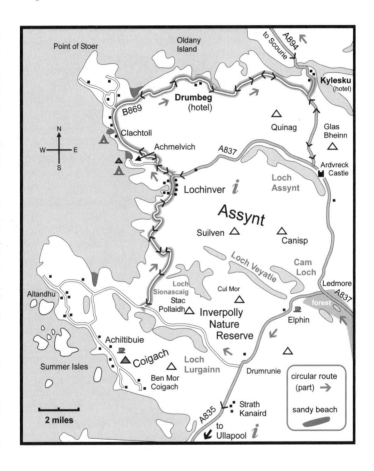

KYLESKU TO DURNESS

Long climbs, with impressive views of lochs, mountains and the sea
Route grading: **Hilly** (36 miles)

These are not quite the biggest mountains in Scotland, but there is no easy option of just following the glen. The Atlantic coast is pierced deeply by the sea, with fjord-like lochs, and the road climbs to get between them.

There are also some fine beaches. You can walk, or possibly mountain bike, to Sandwood Bay. This two-mile stretch of sand might have perhaps two other people on it. There are other fine beaches too, around Durness.

Even if you never leave your bike, you are sure to see plenty of seabirds. The sea cliffs, islands and stacks are filled with birds. A good way to see them might be to cycle to Cape Wrath (page 128). The highest sea cliffs in mainland Britain are here: 920 feet high.

Kylesku, just off the main road, has a hotel doing bar lunches, B&Bs, a toilet, but no food shop. The road is carried over the loch by the Kylesku Bridge, after which it begins a steady climb to the north-west.

There are some great views over Loch a'Chàirn Bhàin, towards the mountain Quinag. After this, you pass Duartmore Forest, and several lochs. There are intermittent views out to the west, towards the Point of Stoer and Oldany Island. After this, there's a descent to Scourie. There is a campsite with a tearoom here, the Scourie Hotel, and a food shop.

Going north from Scourie, you pass a minor road leading to Handa Island Bird Reserve. This is certainly the most spectacular bird reserve in Britain, both from the point of view of the number and variety of birds and the cliff scenery. A regular ferry takes you over. You would need at least four hours on the island. The road to Handa Island is hilly. Just before the junction at Laxford Bridge, there is a view of the mountains Arkle and Foinaven.

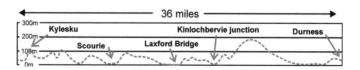

KYLESKU TO DURNESS

We continue north-east, heading towards the junction for Kinlochbervie. There is a hotel at the B801/A838 road junction. Going to Kinlochbervie is a six-mile diversion. Early on, you pass the food shop, the London Store. Kinlochbervie is a fishing port. Food is available in the Fisherman's Mission. Sandwood Bay is a two-mile stretch of beautiful sand, with Atlantic rollers pounding the beach. There are rock pinnacles. It is altogether a remote and lovely place.

The final section to Durness is a lonely stretch of road, with fine views of the quartzite ramparts of the mountain Foinaven. After this, there is a long descent to the sea at the Kyle of Durness. Durness is strung out along the cliff top. There's a tourist office, a youth hostel and a supermarket. Another place to visit is Smoo Cave.

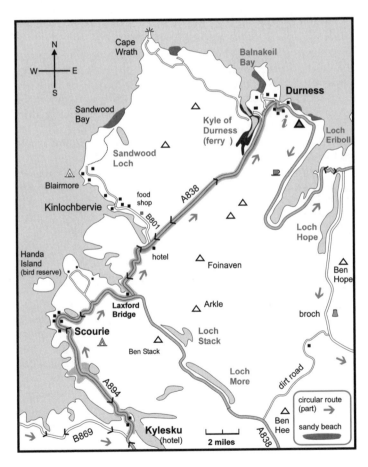

DURNESS TO ALTNAHARRA VIA LOCH HOPE

Long distances here with few food stops – take some
sandwiches!
Route grading: **Varied** (42 miles)

After Durness, the road zigzags past lovely beaches, before
turning south for the long haul round Loch Eriboll. The road
on the west side of the loch is fairly flat for a change but it gets
a bit hillier on the east side, as you work your way north.
Choraidh Farm Park is on the west side of the loch. It has a
tearoom. There are farm animals and a museum showing
crofting life. Perhaps your first priority might be the tearoom!

When you leave Loch Eriboll, there's another climb, then a
descent to the River Hope. This river is only a mile long and
connects Loch Hope to the sea. Turn right immediately after
crossing the river, taking a minor road by the side of the loch.

Ben Hope, Scotland's most northerly Munro (mountain
over 3,000 feet), will be visible most of the time. Shortly after
you leave the loch, you will pass Dun Dornaigil Broch.

Brochs are 2,000-year-old fortified towers, generally built
between 100 BC and AD 100. It has been possible to date them
exactly because sometimes Roman artefacts are found inside.
The Romans conquered England but failed to subdue the
Picts in Scotland. Obviously some trading took place. There is
a theory that brochs were built as a defence against Roman
slave ships.

Shortly after the broch, there is a dirt road connecting to
the A838 just north of Loch Shin, by way of Gobernuisgach
Lodge. A locked gate at its south end prevents its use by cars,
but this is usually no impediment to bikes.

As you approach the junction at Altnaharra, you meet the
Altnaharra Hotel. This is primarily a fishing hotel but they'll
cater for cyclists too. East of here is the austere beauty of
Sutherland's Flow Country, with its endless vistas over
moorland. Here our route meets the National Cycle Network
and you can follow the Route 1 signs to continue south.

DURNESS TO ALTNAHARRA VIA LOCH HOPE

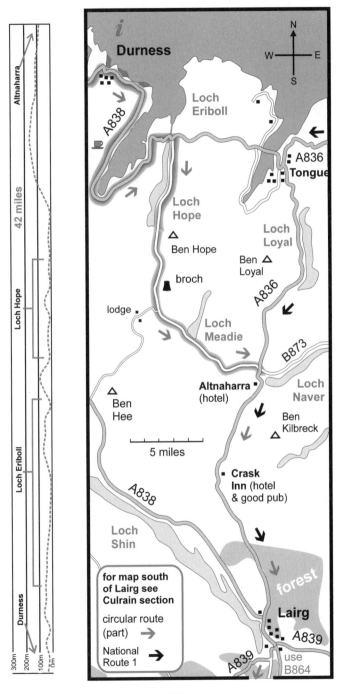

Durness

Loch
Eriboll

A838

A836
Tongue

Loch
Hope

△
Ben Hope

broch

lodge

Loch
Meadie

Loch
Loyal

Ben △
Loyal

A836

B873

Loch
Naver

△
Ben
Hee

Altnaharra
(hotel)

Ben
Kilbreck
△

5 miles

Crask
Inn (hotel
& good pub)

A838

Loch
Shin

forest

Lairg

A839

for map south
of Lairg see
Culrain section

circular route
(part) →

National
Route 1 →

A839

use
B864

Altnaharra

42 miles

Loch Hope

Loch Eriboll

Durness

300m 200m 100m 0m

ALTNAHARRA TO CULRAIN VIA LAIRG

The route rejoins the National Cycle Network for the
final section to Culrain
Route grading: **Varied** (30 miles)

When this route joins the A836 east of Loch Meadie, it meets
National Cycle Route 1 again. From here, you should follow the
Route 1 cycle signs south; this will lead you eventually to
Culrain.

The first part, past hotels at Altnaharra and Crask Inn, is easy
as far as finding your way is concerned, though the pedalling is
more difficult. The Crask Inn is seemingly an old drovers' inn.
They welcome Munro-baggers, long distance walkers, anglers
and, of course, cyclists travelling between Lairg and Altnaharra.
If you want to stay at the inn, bear in mind it has only three
rooms, so be sure to book ahead. The cottage nearby is owned
by the innkeeper and is being fitted out as a bunkhouse.

South of this, the route is more complicated, so some care
is required. Lairg is not especially pretty, but it is a substantial
town, where you should be able to find a bed or a meal. You
can catch trains (which take bikes) from Lairg railway station
to Inverness or Thurso. You'll find it has quite a lot to offer,
including a range of places to eat, drink, shop and stay.

Leave Lairg on the A839, following signs for Ullapool. A
mile after crossing the river, bear left onto the B864.

You follow the B864 for five miles, following the west bank
of the River Shin. The Falls of Shin are worth a look, and
there's a tearoom in the Visitor Centre.

A mile or so after the falls, you meet the A837. Turn left and
cross the river. After a further mile, turn right onto the A836.
Soon after this, you see Carbisdale Castle Youth Hostel on the
other side of the river, usually flying a Scottish flag. This is a
sign you need to leave the A836 at Invershin Station. Cross the
river on the footbridge again, to return to the point you
started from some days ago. The map for this last part is
shown in the Culrain to Ledmore Junction section (page 133).

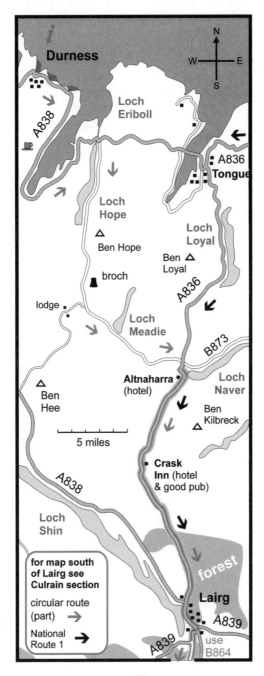

i

Durness

A838

Loch
Eriboll

N
W — E
S

A836
Tongue

Loch
Hope

△
Ben Hope

broch

Loch
Loyal

Ben △
Loyal

A836

lodge

Loch
Meadie

B873

△
Ben
Hee

Altnaharra
(hotel)

Loch
Naver

Ben
Kilbreck
△

5 miles

**Crask
Inn** (hotel
& good pub)

A838

Loch
Shin

forest

for map south
of Lairg see
Culrain section

circular route
(part) →

National
Route 1 →

Lairg

A839

A839

use
B864

ARRAN AND THE WESTERN ISLANDS

DISTANCES AND ROUTE GRADING

CHAPTER 6

ARRAN AND THE WESTERN ISLANDS

This chapter covers the islands of the west coast of Scotland. That is, the Outer Hebrides, normally called the Western Isles; plus Skye, Mull, Jura, Islay and Arran. The cycle routes on the Isle of Mull also take in adjacent parts of the mainland (Ardnamurchan and Morvern). The Isle of Bute is on page 102.

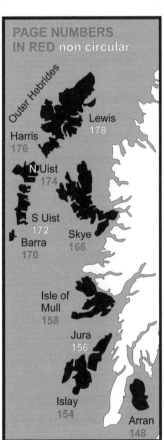

PAGE NUMBERS
IN RED non circular

Outer Hebrides

Lewis
178

Harris
176

N Uist
174

S Uist
172

Barra
170

Skye
166

Isle of Mull
158

Jura
156

Islay
154

Arran
148

Scotland has nearly 800 islands but only 130 are inhabited. Of these, perhaps 13 have enough roads to be of interest to cyclists, but this still allows plenty of scope. Mull, for example, would take several days to explore fully on a bike.

The best thing about these islands is their quiet; the rhythm of life is gentler. The scenery is varied but, from the wild coast of Lewis to the mountains of Arran, invariably beautiful.

With the exception of Skye, all the islands require the use of a ferry to reach them. At the time of writing, the ferry operator, Caledonian MacBrayne, still had a monopoly on the Western Isles. See the Appendix for more information.

ISLE OF ARRAN

Brodick – Sannox – Lochranza
Route grading: **Hilly** (14 miles)

You'll know this is the right place when you get on the ferry –
quite often in summer, the bikes outnumber the cars. When
you start to cycle, you'll find a bit of traffic between Brodick
and Whiting Bay – other than that, no problem. If you listed
the most attractive features of Scotland, then tried to squeeze
them all onto one medium-sized island, you'd end up with
Arran.

Turn right after leaving the ferry terminal, shops, hotels
and tearooms on the left, with the sea on your right. After a
mile, you will be clear of the town. You'll pass the Arran
Heritage Museum on the right. Shortly after this is the left
turn for The String road, which crosses the centre of the
island to the west coast and Blackwaterfoot. An alternative way
of going to Lochranza is to cycle over The String, then cycle
up the west coast (see diagram below).

Brodick Castle is mostly Victorian but parts date from the
thirteenth century. There's a lovely wooded garden, with
masses of rhododendrons, and a nature trail with a path
leading to Goat Fell. The castle has collections of paintings,
furniture and porcelain. The Dukes of Hamilton liked to
shoot things, as you can tell by the number of stags' heads in
the hall. After the castle, you cycle along by a rocky coastline
to reach the village of Corrie (shop and hotel).

Continue north again, by the sea, to Sannox. The golf club
tearoom here is open to passers-by. You will need some extra
calories for the climb afterwards. The road from Sannox
sweeps round to the north-west, climbing to 200 metres,
before dropping down to Lochranza. There are views of the
mountain ridges.

Lochranza is a pretty village with a castle by the loch, a
shop, a hotel, a distillery (restaurant) and a café. The youth
hostel here is a lovely old house. Lochranza is also the

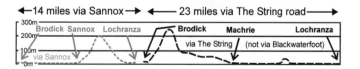

terminal for the summer ferry to Claonaig on Kintyre. A short cycle can connect this to another ferry crossing to the islands of Islay, Jura and Colonsay (see following pages).

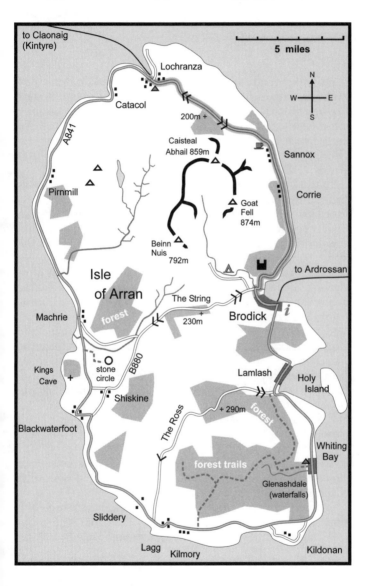

ISLE OF ARRAN

Lochranza to Blackwaterfoot
Route grading: **Easy** (17 miles)

Continuing round, we pass pretty Catacol Bay. While the road on the east coast was lush and sheltered, the road on the west is more exposed but has a beauty of its own, as it runs past long gravel beaches with the Kintyre Peninsula opposite. Seals are often seen here. The road is flat where it runs beside the sea. There are a few short hills between Machrie and Blackwaterfoot.

Starting at Lochranza in the morning, the tearoom at Pirnmill is probably the best place for morning coffee. Alternatively, the golf club at Machrie, seven miles on, can usually provide some. At Machrie, a minor road with good views connects to The String road, enabling you to cut the corner to go to Brodick via The String.

Just south of Machrie, off the coast road, immediately after Machrie Water, is Machrie Stone Circle. This Neolithic monument is along a rough track. It is impressive and stands in a fine location.

Just south of this again is another historic remnant, the King's Cave, with its legendary association with Robert the Bruce, King of Scots and victor over Edward II at Bannockburn. It also has Pictish and early Christian carvings. The caves are in a cliff, isolated from the sea by a raised beach.

The next village south is Blackwaterfoot, western end of The String road. It has a hotel that does bar lunches, a small harbour and a food shop. The hotel has an indoor swimming pool that is open to passers-by.

Arran is cut in half by the Highland Boundary Fault, a geological division that makes the north rugged and hilly, whereas the south is more gentle and lower-lying. This non-hilly aspect does not apply to the roads in the south of the island, however.

Wildlife includes deer, pheasant, otter and eagle frequently

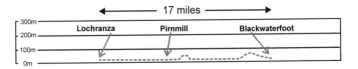

seen in the hills. There are colonies of seals near coastal caves. Arran means peaked island in Gaelic.

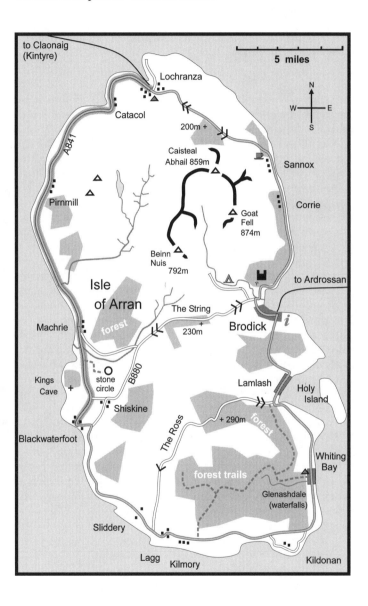

ISLE OF ARRAN

Blackwaterfoot – Whiting Bay – Brodick
Route grading: **Hilly** (25 miles)

You can cut some of the hilly coast road by using The Ross to get to Lamlash, but this climbs to 290m. The coast road is the prettier of the two road routes.

There is a tearoom at Lagg, and hotels providing food near Kilmory and Kildonan. The one at Kildonan, which is on a loop off the main road, has a view of the rocky islet of Pladda.

Another option is to bike the forest trails to Whiting Bay. You pass Glenashdale Falls, which are worth seeing. Access to the trails is from a signposted track leading north-east, one kilometre east of Kilmory. If you are starting from Whiting Bay, follow the Glenashdale Falls sign by the bowling green.

Going round the coast, you enter Whiting Bay, which has tearooms, B&Bs, hotels and a youth hostel. The coast road between Whiting Bay and Brodick is not particularly quiet and is fairly hilly.

Going north again, you enter Lamlash, with Holy Island opposite. Holy Island is occupied by Buddhists but it was called Holy Island before this; it derives its name from Saint Molaise, who lived on the island in the sixth century. There is a ferry, and tours of the Buddhist monastery are available, so allow several hours if you decide to visit it. Out of Lamlash, it's another stiff climb to get to Brodick and complete the circle.

Ferry times from Ardrossan: 0700, 0945, 1230, 1515, 1800, 2030. Sundays: 0945, 1230, 1515, 1800. From Brodick: 0820, 1105, 1350, 1640, 1920. Sundays: 1105, 1350, 1640, 1920.

The Lochranza–Claonaig ferry runs April–October, from about 9 a.m. to 8 p.m., at 75-minute intervals. To confirm times phone: 01294 463470.

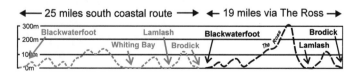

ISLE OF ARRAN

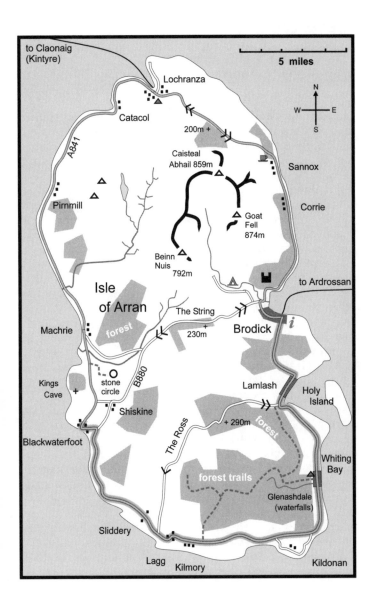

ISLE OF ISLAY

Bird life, malt whisky, great beaches
Route grading: **Varied** (37 miles)

Islay is famous for bird life, malt whisky, and peace and quiet. In many ways, it's the ideal cycling island. The hills are mostly modest, the roads quiet, and everyone you meet seems to smile and say hello. Islay is particularly fertile. Otters and seals are likely to be seen. There are many historical things to look at and miles of lovely beaches.

Caledonian MacBrayne sails from Kennacraig, on the Kintyre Peninsula, every day of the week. This is convenient if coming from Arran, as Claonaig, where the ferry from Lochranza terminates, is only seven miles away on the other side of the peninsula.

There are two different arrival points in Islay: Port Ellen and Port Askaig. The ferry from Kennacraig calls at one or the other, but not both. Port Askaig is an interesting way to arrive, as you sail up the narrow channel between Islay and Jura. Arriving at Port Ellen gives a sea view of the distilleries of Laphroaig, Ardbeg and Lagavulin.

There is no lack of distilleries on Islay. It can be a surprise to the malt whisky drinker, who has seen labels such as Bunnahabhainn on bottles in bars from Sydney to Seattle, to discover that these are actually places as well. The shock can be tempered, though, by a visit to the establishment concerned, who will administer the elixir, usually free of charge, and let you look around (phone first).

Which routes you take to explore the island will very much depend on where you are staying. Port Charlotte is a good location and there is a comfortable youth hostel there, as well as a wildlife centre and tearoom. Bridgend, further east, is more centrally located. There is a hotel that does bar lunches and a good food shop.

Probably the best cycle on Islay is around the western peninsula, between Bridgend and Portnahaven. Start at either

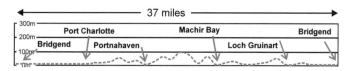

Bridgend or Port Charlotte and cycle south-west on the A847 to Portnahaven. Portnahaven is a pretty harbour village. The rocky islet of Orsay is opposite, with its lighthouse. There is a coffee shop and a tiny bar in the village.

Leave Portnahaven on the minor road which goes up the west coast. You pass a stone circle after three miles. Soon after that, the road turns south again towards Port Charlotte. If you want to do a little more, leave the surfaced road at this point, turning left to a rough track that goes steeply up a hill. This leads to the beautiful beach at Machir Bay. Bike or walk to the public road on the north side of the bay, then continue round to Loch Gorm and Loch Gruinart. There is a bird reserve near here.

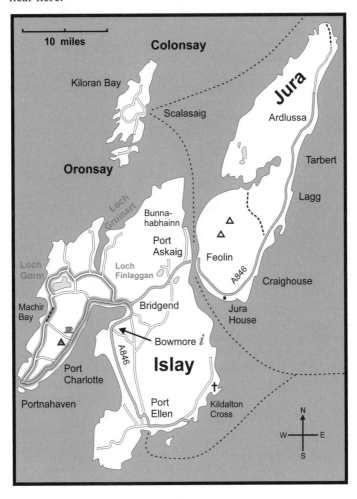

JURA, COLONSAY AND ORONSAY

Only one road, the A846, which has grass in the middle
Route grading: **Hilly** (35 miles)

The island of Jura is more of a wilderness than Islay.
Mountainous and with only one road, a mountain bike is more
suitable for exploring to the north tip. Jura has about 5,000
deer and 250 people; indeed, the name Jura means deer island.
Colonsay can be an attractive day trip from Jura, although you
must first go to Islay (via shuttle ferry) to get the
Islay–Colonsay ferry, which sails on a Wednesday.

Access to Jura is by a frequent ferry from Port Askaig (on
Islay) to Feolin. There is no direct ferry from the Scottish
mainland. There are several places to stay: the Jura Hotel, a
bothy and a few B&Bs. There are no campsites and the estate
tends to discourage camper vans. Cycle-campers should not
have any problem.

A bike is the ideal way to get around on Jura. The only road
is the A846, mainly a narrow strip of tarmac, often with grass
in the middle. This deteriorates as you go north, into a poor
road, a rough track and then a footpath. Near the northern tip
is the Gulf of Corryvreckan, the site of a famous whirlpool. It
is said to be the second-largest in the world. On the way to
this, you will pass lonely Kinnachdrachd, where George
Orwell wrote the novel *1984*.

Craighouse is the only significant settlement on the island.
It is in an attractive situation, overlooking Small Isles Bay. The
Jura Hotel is here, along with two B&Bs, the distillery and a
food shop. Jura House, near the southern tip of the island, is
worth visiting. This has a walled garden with exotic plants and
an attractive tea tent. There are a number of walks nearby.

You can travel to Colonsay from Oban but it is also possible
to take a day trip on a Wednesday from Islay. This gives you
about six hours on the island, which is enough to explore all
the roads. For a clockwise trip, take the first left after the
harbour. You could call at the café at the harbour first. They

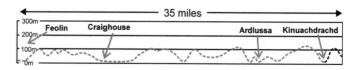

might know the state of the tide. This is necessary if you are going to the adjacent island of Oronsay, as you won't want to be cut off. There is about a kilometre of wet sand to cross. Oransay has a ruined priory, with some interesting relics.

On Colonsay, continue clockwise round the island, passing coastal scenery and some lochs. Near Colonsay House, there is an interesting detour to Kiloran Bay, one of the finest beaches in the Western Isles. Complete the circuit on the public road or detour through the grounds of Colonsay House – don't miss the ferry!

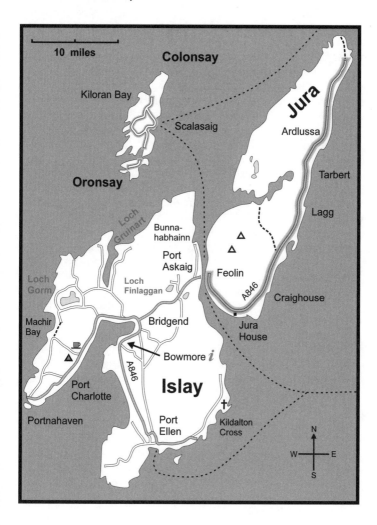

ARDNAMURCHAN AND THE ISLE OF MULL

Morvern to Calgary Bay (Mull)
Route grading: **Hilly** (103 miles, see next page)

For most people, this will be a two- or three-day cycle ride. The route is circular, with two ferry crossings. The scenery is spectacular but the roads are hilly, particularly so between Dervaig and Tobermory. Most of the roads in this route are single track with passing places. Another Mull route is described after this one. It would be worthwhile combining them to spend a week in the area. May is a good time to go, as the weather is often fine and the road traffic will be light.

The route begins at the junction of the A861 and the B8043, six miles south-west of the Corran ferry. There is nothing at this junction. The Corran ferry is ten miles south-west of Fort William. Morvern is surprisingly quiet and quite beautiful. The B8043 climbs over a hill initially, passing some lochs, then descends to the shore of Loch Linnhe. It passes the little church at Kingairloch before it begins a climb inland. The church is worth seeing before you begin the climb. There is a further climb after the B8043/A884 junction but you are soon flying down the hill towards Lochaline. Lochaline has a shop, a hotel and a fast-food stall by the ferry terminal in summer.

On Mull, turn right onto the A849. This is a normal road, but beyond Salen, the route is on single track roads, with passing places. The village of Salen has a hotel doing bar food, a supermarket, a tearoom and B&Bs. There is no source of food on the B8073 between Salen and Calgary Bay.

There is a small climb to get from Salen to the west coast of Mull, then you turn right to the B8073 to cycle round the north side of Loch na Keal. There are spectacular views of the cliffs on the other side. The ferry to Ulva is at the most obvious point (see map). The farmer on Ulva runs a restaurant and there is some excellent mountain biking. You are not allowed to cycle on the adjacent island of Gometra.

On Mull itself, as you work past Ulva going west, you pass an impressive waterfall plunging over the sea cliffs. The road winds up and down then begins its major climb over to Calgary Bay. As you descend to Calgary Bay, there is a panoramic view of the islands of Eigg, Rum and the Cuillin Mountains on Skye.

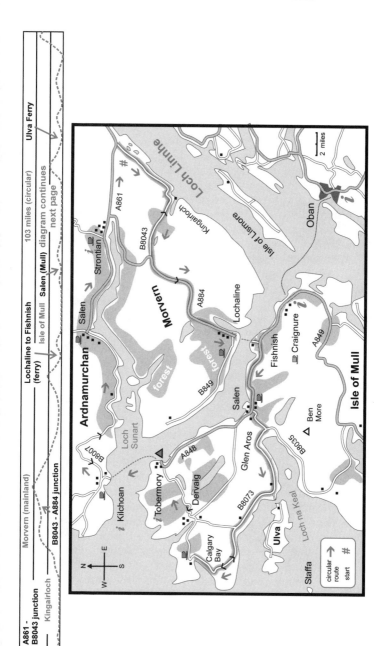

ARDNAMURCHAN AND THE ISLE OF MULL

Calgary Bay (Mull) to Morvern
Route grading: **Hilly** (103 miles)

After Calgary Bay, the climb over to Dervaig is easy enough. The climb after that, between Dervaig and Tobermory, could not be called easy. There is a hotel in Dervaig just before the start of the climb.

After that, there are more ups and downs before you finally plunge into Tobermory. Tobermory is one of the most photographed places in Scotland. We catch the ferry to Kilchoan here. There are all kinds of places to eat, drink and sleep (including a youth hostel).

If you are intending to cycle from Kilchoan to the Corran ferry in one day, you need to catch an early ferry from Tobermory. This ferry operates only in the summer. There is a tearoom and a hotel shortly after disembarking in Ardnamurchan, but no refreshment stops after that until you get to Salen.

As usual, the route begins with a climb. At the top, you get a splendid view of the Isle of Rum to the north. There's an undulating section, then a descent towards Loch Sunart, with amazing views. It's probably best to stop if you want to admire the scenery.

Fairly soon, you arrive at sea level – but if you think the hills are over, you will soon be disillusioned. The road winds up and down, keeping close to the shore of the loch much of the time. There is lots of woodland, Scots pine, rhododendron, birch and oak, with frequent views across the loch to Morvern.

There is a shop and a hotel in Salen. The hotel has tables outside, overlooking the loch. Strontian has a supermarket, several hotels and numerous B&Bs. At this point, you finally leave Loch Sunart and climb over Glen Tarbert to get to Loch Linnhe. The last section to the ferry at Corran is definitely flat! There is another route in this area in the Northern Highlands chapter of this book (page 120).

ARDNAMURCHAN AND THE ISLE OF MULL

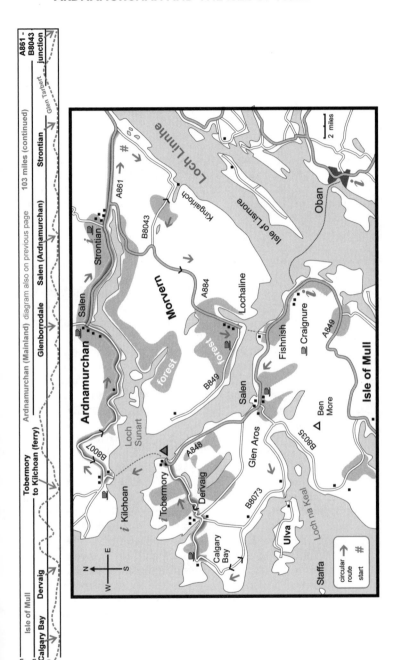

300m
200m
100m
0m

Isle of Mull

Calgary Bay   Dervaig

Tobermory
to Kilchoan (ferry)

Ardnamurchan (Mainland) diagram also on previous page

Glenborrodale   Salen (Ardnamurchan)

103 miles (continued)

Strontian

Glen Tarbert

A861 –
B8043
junction

161

LISMORE AND THE ISLE OF MULL

South Ballachulish to Ulva ferry (Mull)
Route grading: **Hilly** (132 miles)

This is a three- or four-day ride, circular with four ferry crossings. The route has a four-mile section on the A82 between the Corran Ferry and South Ballachulish. If you have a car, it might be worth using it to avoid these busy four miles. Apart from this, much of the route is on single track roads with passing places. May is a good time to go, as the road traffic will be light.

Start at the junction of the A82 and the A828, south of the Ballachulish Bridge. You could ride down Glen Coe to start. Early in the morning this is fine, later on heavy traffic makes it inadvisable. The A828 is quieter than the A82; there are views across to Morvern. You see Castle Stalker on an island on the right. A mile after this, take a right turn to a minor road for Port Appin. A foot passenger ferry takes you over to Lismore. If you are not intending to stay overnight on Lismore, catch this ferry no later than 2 p.m. There is a shop and seafood restaurant in Port Appin.

Don't delay in Lismore, as there is no evening ferry. The ferry to Oban is a left turn after five miles, signed 'Achnacroish Pier'. Oban is the departure point for ferries going to the Western Isles. You can arrive there from Lismore and depart for Mull without leaving the ferry terminal. There are two bike shops in Oban.

Craignure, on Mull, has a couple of hotels and a food shop. Turn left to the A849 after leaving the ferry. You pass Duart Castle, then descend to Lochdon. There's a climb to take you over to Loch Spelve before you begin a major climb over Glen More. There is a hotel providing food a mile or so beyond the A849/B8035 junction. There is a food shop next to it.

The B8035 rolls along by the shore then climbs over the Ardmeanach Peninsula to get to the spectacular sea inlet of Loch na Keal. There are wonderful views of Staffa, Ulva and Little Colonsay. Following this, the route takes you round Loch na Keal. The road on the south is flat but there is a climb on the north side just before Ulva. The village of Salen is slightly off-route. It has a hotel doing bar food, a supermarket, a tearoom and B&Bs.

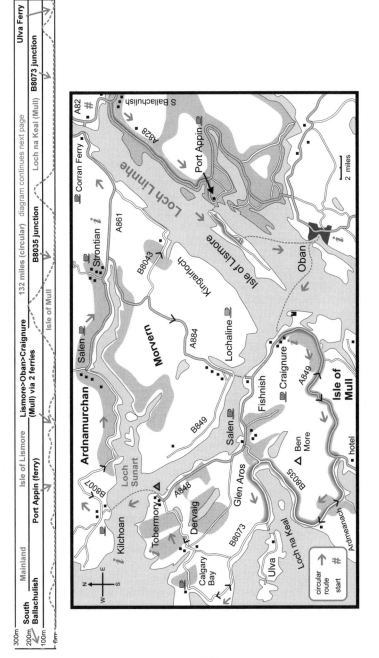

LISMORE AND THE ISLE OF MULL

Ulva ferry (Mull) to South Ballachulish
Route grading: **Hilly** (132 miles)

The ferry to Ulva is at the most obvious point (see map, opposite). The farmer on the island also runs a restaurant and there is some good mountain biking. You are not allowed to cycle on the adjacent island of Gometra.

On Mull itself, as you work past Ulva going west, you pass an impressive waterfall plunging over the sea cliffs. The road winds up and down then begins its major climb over to Calgary Bay. There is a short cut but this is fiendishly steep and, in any case, misses out the beautiful bay.

As you descend to Calgary Bay, there is a panoramic view of the islands of Eigg, Rum and the Cuillin Mountains on Skye. Linger on the sands or visit the gallery and restaurant just beyond, which offers a wide choice of food. After Calgary Bay, the climb over to Dervaig is easy enough. The climb after that, between Dervaig and Tobermory, could not be called easy. There is a hotel in Dervaig, just before the start of the climb. After that, there are more ups and downs before you finally plunge into Tobermory.

If you are intending to cycle from Kilchoan to the Corran ferry in one day, you need to catch an early ferry from Tobermory. This ferry operates only in the summer. There is a tearoom and a hotel shortly after disembarking but no refreshment stops after that until you get to Salen.

As usual, the route begins with a climb, at the top of which you get a splendid view of Rum. There's un undulating section, then a descent towards Loch Sunart, with amazing views. Fairly soon, you arrive at sea level – but if you think the hills are over, you will soon be disillusioned. The road winds up and down, keeping close to the shore of the loch much of the time. The road runs through woodland, Scots pine, rhododendron, birch and oak, with frequent views across the loch to Morvern.

There is a shop and a hotel in Salen. The hotel has tables outside. Strontian has a supermarket, several hotels and numerous B&Bs. At this point, you finally leave Loch Sunart and climb over Glen Tarbert to get to Loch Linnhe. The last section to the ferry at Corran is definitely flat!

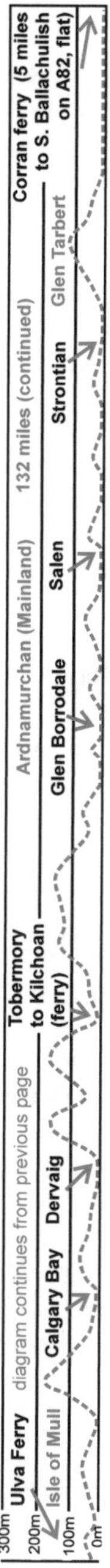
300m
200m
100m
0m
Ulva Ferry
Isle of Mull
diagram continues from previous page
Calgary Bay
Dervaig
Tobermory to Kilchoan (ferry)
Ardnamurchan (Mainland)
Glen Borrodale
Salen
132 miles (continued)
Strontian
Glen Tarbert
Corran ferry (5 miles to S. Ballachulish on A82, flat)

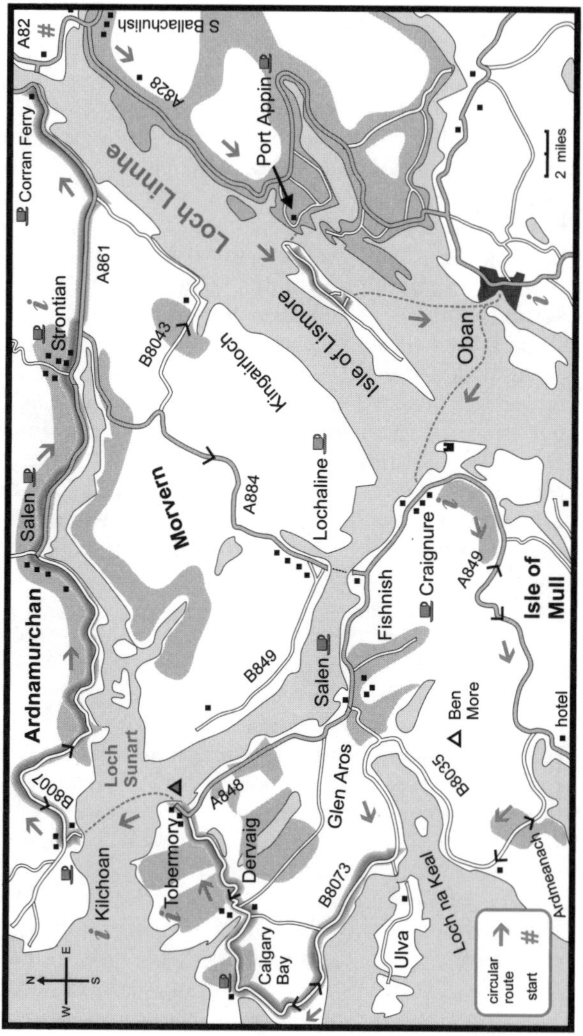
Loch Linnhe
S Ballachulish
A82
A828
Port Appin
Corran Ferry
A861
Strontian
B8043
Kingairloch
Isle of Lismore
Oban
Lochaline
A884
Morvern
Salen
Ardnamurchan
B8007
Loch Sunart
Kilchoan
Tobermory
A848
Dervaig
B8073
Calgary Bay
Glen Aros
Salen
B849
Fishnish
Craignure
A849
Isle of Mull
Ben More
B8035
hotel
Ardmeanach
Loch na Keal
Ulva
2 miles
N
E
S
W
circular route
start

ISLE OF SKYE – SLEAT PENINSULA

A very beautiful and very hilly short circular – good views
of the mountain Bla Bheinn
Route grading: **Hilly** (16 miles)

This short circular gives excellent views of the impressive
mountain Bla Bheinn (Blaven). On the way, there is some
beautiful coastline and natural woodland.

If you have a motor vehicle, a good place to start is at the
northern junction, where there is a small area convenient for
parking. After this, go south towards Armadale on the A851,
then turn right after Teangue, signed 'Tarskavaig'. There is a
steady climb to 188 metres, then a fast scenic descent past
Loch Dhughaill to Tarskavaig Bay.

After this, there is a smaller climb over to Tarskavaig (take
either fork), then a drop to the sea near Tokavaig. Here you
get your first really good view of the impressive ridges of Bla
Bheinn. This is now owned by the John Muir Trust, which was
established to conserve wild places. On a headland near here is
Dunscaith Castle, though it is difficult to see, as it's so ruined
that it appears a natural formation. Here, in legend, the
warrior queen of Skye is said to have taught the Irish hero,
Cuchulainn, the art of war.

After this, there is another climb and a descent to the sea at
Ord, where there is a hotel. The return to the A851 isn't such
a severe climb, just 113 metres this time.

The woodland at Tokavaig is a nature reserve extending to
over 100 acres. It stands on a limestone outcrop that is much
more fertile than the surrounding rocks. In summer, there will
be purple orchids and primroses. The trees are ash, birch, hazel,
bird cherry and hawthorn. The birds will include chaffinch,
willow warbler, wren, mistle-thrush and robin.

Most of Sleat is owned by two private estates. The southern
half is owned by the Clan Donald Trust – a private charitable
trust with a Visitor Centre at Armadale. The northern half is
owned by Sir Iain Noble, with an office at Isle Ornsay.

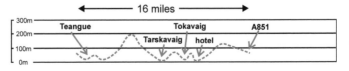

Crofting is a way of life here. Each crofter lives in a crofthouse, on a five- to ten-acre croft, usually rented at a nominal fee from a landlord. There are grazing rights over communal lands. Crofting is intimately connected to the Highland language, culture and history. All the same, modern crofters have a lifestyle that crofters of 100 years ago could hardly imagine.

Sleat is traditionally called the garden of Skye, because parts of it are quite fertile and its east coast is sheltered from the worst of the Atlantic gales by the rest of Skye. There is a Gaelic college at Ostaig, and a visitor centre at Armadale Castle, just south of this route.

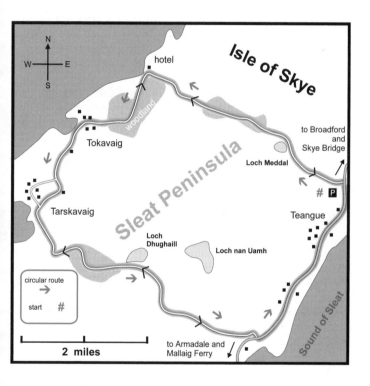

ISLE OF SKYE – TROTTERNISH

A loop through the dramatic scenery of Skye's northern peninsula
Route grading: **Hilly** (49 miles)

This loop around the dramatic Trotternish Peninsula begins and ends in Portree – the capital of the Isle of Skye. The route explores one of the most scenic parts of Skye, yet it is rarely all that busy.

Leave Portree by the A855. There is a climb out of the town then a drop to the picturesque Storr lochs, where there are views north to the rock pinnacle of the Old Man of Storr.

Continue past the cliffs of Kilt Rock to the village of Staffin, often with views over the sea to the Torridon Mountains on the mainland. Near Staffin there is a possible short cut (see map, opposite) but this involves a climb from sea level of over 260 metres. This could also be the basis for a shorter (half-day?) northern circular route.

After Staffin, the road winds below the cliffs of the Quirang then turns west then south down the other side of the peninsula. There are views of the Outer Hebrides. After passing the crofting communities at Kilmuir, you drop into the village of Uig, which hugs the shore of a deep bay.

The return to Portree follows the A87 at first. Ten miles south of Uig, just beyond the village and white church at Kensaleyre, turn right onto the B8036, which cuts across to the A850. On reaching the A850, turn left and after a half mile turn right onto the minor road to Benness. This road takes a quiet route back into Portree.

Much of the traffic on the A87 is going to and from the Outer Hebrides ferries at Uig, which only run a couple of times a day, so it is worth checking the ferry times and planning your day accordingly, to give you a quiet run south from Uig.

The Quirang is an area of screes and rock pinnacles. It was the setting for Bonnie Prince Charlie's last days in Scotland. In 1746, with the help of Flora MacDonald, he disguised himself as 'Betty Burke' and escaped from the Outer Hebrides to Skye. He then made his way to Portree, where he said a final goodbye to Flora. The room where they parted is now part of the Royal Hotel. Flora was arrested and sent to the Tower of London.

Later she married and emigrated to America, returning to Scotland in 1779. Flora's cottage at Flodigarry is now restored and provides hotel accommodation. A memorial marks her final resting place at Duntulm. This memorial is a replacement, the earlier one having been entirely removed piece by piece by tourists.

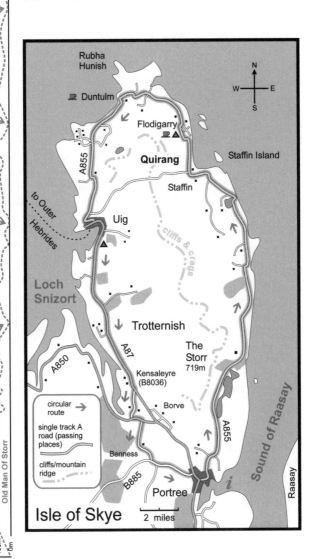

Isle of Skye

2 miles

OUTER HEBRIDES – ISLE OF BARRA

A coastal circular, great beaches – a few hills too!
Route grading: **Varied** (14 miles)

This is a short circular route on the southern island of Barra. It would also be a good start on the first day of a longer tour.

Traditionally, touring cyclists do the Outer Hebrides (Barra, South Uist, Benbecula, North Uist, Harris and Lewis) as a long chain of islands, taking perhaps a week to cycle the whole thing. The scenery is at times so beautiful it defies description.

Barra is quite hilly, with sandy beaches on the west coast. Exploring on a bike would take a day. The best beach is at Tangasdale (Tangasdal in Gaelic). You could cycle over to Vatersay on the causeway. This was built after the local bull drowned on his annual swim to impregnate the cows of Vatersay.

If you are going north on a bike, take it on the council-run car ferry from Eoligarry (Eolaigearraidh) to Eriskay. It's also possible to travel from Castlebay (Barra) to Lochboisdale (South Uist) on the Caledonian MacBrayne ferry. Caledonian MacBrayne will also be running the small ferry between Barra and Eriskay (for South Uist) in 2004. Check for any changes (01878 700 288).

If you are arriving in Barra from Oban, you'll probably be cycling down the Cal-Mac gangplank around 8 p.m. and the immediate need will be to find a bed. The tourist office opens to meet the ferry, but if you want an economical B&B, it might be best to book first. Dunard Hostel (01871 810443) is an independent hostel in Castlebay. It's two minutes' cycle from the ferry terminal. There are several hotels and shops in this area.

There aren't many Gaelic words that have made it into English but 'machair' is one. It means land behind the beach. These islands have lots of beaches: quiet stretches of sand deposited by countless Atlantic rollers. The fertility of the

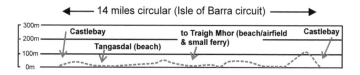

14 miles circular (Isle of Barra circuit)

machair is due to a mixture of peat (which is normally infertile, due to poor drainage) and windblown sand. In summer, you will notice many wild flowers. The scenery in the Outer Hebrides is amongst the most beautiful in the world, and the sea is very clear. On a sunny day, when it covers the white sands of the west coast, it has more colours of blue and green than you can imagine. The white colour of the sand is due to its high shell content (over 80 per cent). The marine life includes dolphins, seals, sharks and whales. The Minch (between Skye and the Outer Hebrides) is one of the best areas in Britain for whale-watching. Seals are particularly common and will be seen sunning themselves all round the islands. Not surprisingly, the Outer Hebrides are also famous for shellfish, which thrive in the unpolluted waters.

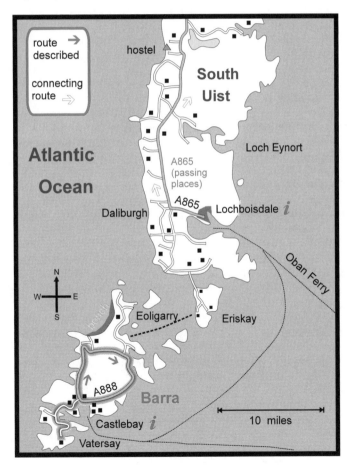

OUTER HEBRIDES – SOUTH UIST TO BENBECULA

Connecting the islands
Route grading: **Easy** (25 miles)

Two issues arise if you are planning to cycle the Outer Hebrides: which direction to do it in, and how to get there. The ferry journeys will be from Oban to Castlebay (on Barra) and Lewis (on Stornoway) to Ullapool.

Which direction to cycle in depends upon wind direction. The prevailing wind is from the south-west, although in summer there are sometimes northerly winds. The northerly winds are likely to be dry, but westerly winds might bring rain. A possible problem is that the two mainland ferry terminals – Oban and Mallaig – are 100 miles apart: so if you leave a vehicle at one of these places, you have a 100-mile cycle on busy roads to return to it.

One solution would be to get the train. You can travel by train to Oban but the nearest train station to Ullapool is at Culrain, 50 miles to the east. Cycling between Culrain and Ullapool is fine (pages 132–5) and the scenery is splendid. Most people could do it in a day.

Causeways join South Uist, Benbecula and North Uist. The car ferry terminal for South Uist is at Lochboisdale, though you might miss this out if you are cycling north from Barra. There is a food shop and a hotel providing bar food at the junction at Daliburgh (Dalabrog). The road has a few easy hills as it works north. There are possible diversions west on lovely little back roads and you might like to include these loops in your route, if you can manage a few extra miles.

It's worth noting that there are regular bus services on the islands and that the drivers are usually quite obliging and will take bikes. This could be useful if there is a strong headwind or if it starts to rain! There is a small hostel/bunkhouse at Howmore, for which you will need a sleeping bag. The nearest shop is a mile away. In May, you would not have too much

26 miles Lochboisdale to Gramasdail ←→ 7 miles

300m
200m — Daliburgh (road junction)   North Benbecula (Gramasdail)   small   Daliburgh
Lochboisdale   S. Uist to Benbecula   ferry   (road
100m   causeway   junction)
0m

trouble finding a B&B, but booking in advance would be advisable during the school holidays. I've generally found that most B&B owners, even if full up, will be able to suggest that Mrs so-and-so further up the road might have a space. They might even phone for you.

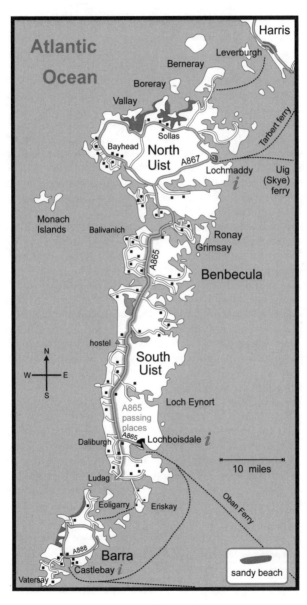

OUTER HEBRIDES – BENBECULA TO NORTH UIST

Connecting the islands
Route grading: **Easy** (27 miles)
(20 miles to Lochmaddy)

Benbecula is not quite as pretty as the other islands but there is a lovely little loop you can do on the island of Grimsay just north of it. The settlement of Baile Mhanaich (Balivanich on older maps) has a good choice of shops and places to buy food.

North Uist is an equal mixture of land, lochs and beaches. Near Lochmaddy, it seems as if there is more water than land – and that doesn't include the sea! Seen from the A865, the beaches in the west are not particularly attractive – but go a little further west, for example to the bird reserve at Balranald, and they are really beautiful.

The beaches in the north, opposite Harris, are more accessible and are equally wonderful. Particularly so is Vallay Strand, with its long finger of sand stretching out towards Boreray, and Vallay Island in the bay.

You should cycle round the whole of North Uist. The northerly spur, leading to the ferry from Berneray to Leverburgh on Harris, is worth cycling even if you don't catch the ferry. This ferry is now run by Caledonian MacBrayne. There is a tourist office at Lochmaddy. Lochmaddy also has a choice of food shops, several hotels doing bar food and a number of B&Bs. Caledonian MacBrayne have a car ferry service from Lochmaddy to Uig on Skye.

There is a thatched blackhouse-style hostel on the Isle of Berneray, quite near to the ferry terminal for Harris. There are also two hostels in North Uist – Uist Outdoor Centre (Lochmaddy) and Taigh Mo Sheanair (Baleshare).

The Outer Hebrides are generally notable for numerous lochs. Some of these are brackish and others are dark and acidic. Water lilies are quite common and many have populations of trout and charr. Birds include dunlin, redshank, plover and

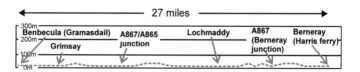

lapwing, and the islands are the last stronghold of the corncrake. Nearly every beach seems to have a population of sandpipers. The islands are formed on one of the oldest exposed types of rock in the world, Lewisian Gneiss. This is grey-coloured, with bands of white and dark minerals contorted by the pressure of the earth. These were formed over 3,000 million years ago. Similar rocks are found today in Canada, to which this part of Scotland was once joined.

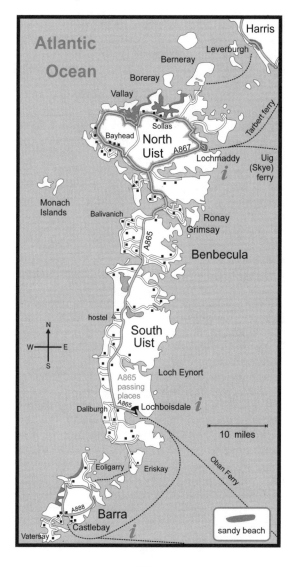

OUTER HEBRIDES – NORTH UIST TO HARRIS (TARBERT)

Connecting the islands
Route grading: **Varied** (22 miles)

Possibly the best place to arrive in Harris is at Leverburgh. Named after soap magnate Lord Leverhulme, it's nothing special, but you will have come from North Uist via lovely Berneray. Ahead on the west is a vast stretch of shell sand: Scarista Beach.

The road on the west coast of South Harris is not too hilly, running through the machair. You pass the island of Taransay. Shortly after this, there is a steady climb of about three miles. At the end of the climb, the road turns north again, going directly to Tarbert.

If you'd like to get a flavour of the east coast, turn right at the top of the hill and go to Tarbert via the Golden Road. Along the way, you'll pass a place where you can see Harris Tweed being woven.

The east coast of Harris is rocky and barren but with little coves and hundreds of small lochans full of water lilies. At the south end is St Clement's Church at Rodel. Dating from the sixteenth century, it has some outstanding medieval stone carvings. The east-coast road twists and turns past small hamlets perched on the Lewisian Gneiss that these islands are made from. Lewissian Gneiss is one of the oldest exposed types of rock in the world. The road is rarely flat. Tarbert has B&Bs, shops, several hotels, an independent hostel and a tourist information office.

Harris Tweed (or 'Clo Mhor' in the original Gaelic, meaning 'the big cloth') is cloth that has been hand-woven by the islanders of Lewis, Harris, Uist and Barra in their homes, using wool that has been dyed and spun in the Outer Hebrides.

As the Industrial Revolution reached Scotland, the mainland turned to mechanisation but the outer islands

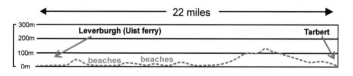

retained their traditional processes. Lewis and Harris had long been known for the excellence of the weaving done there but, up to the middle of the nineteenth century, the cloth was produced mainly for home use or for a local market. More of the cloth is, in fact, produced in Lewis but you can still see Harris tweed being woven in Harris on the west coast at Luskentyre – take the dead-end road off to Luskentyre beach to get there.

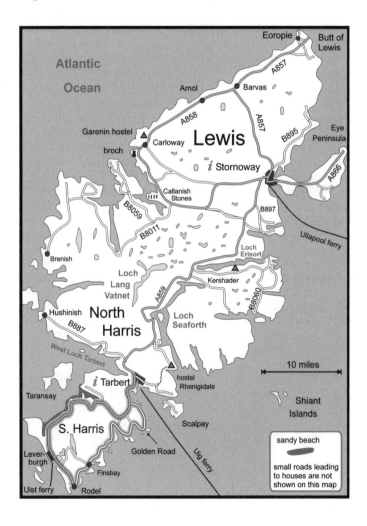

OUTER HEBRIDES – HARRIS (TARBERT) TO LEWIS (STORNOWAY)

Connecting the islands
Route grading: **Hilly** (38 miles)

Going north from Tarbert to Stornoway is a one-day ride, passing fjord-like Loch Seaforth. At first, it's hilly, with a mountainscape more like Norway than Scotland. Just after you pass West Loch Tarbert, there is a long, steep climb. The views are splendid when you get to the top, stretching over towards Rhenigidale and Loch Seaforth.

Naturally, there is a corresponding descent (or climb) on the other side. Once you have passed Loch Seaforth, the cycling gets easier. As in the Uists, you will find that there are regular bus services, with fairly obliging bus drivers who are willing to take bikes.

Harris and Lewis, though named separately, are a single island. Harris is mountainous but scenic. Lewis is mostly open moorland.

Many loch names in Lewis end in 'vat', revealing their Norse origin. The west coast is interesting, with many things to see, notably the broch at Dun Carloway two miles south of Carloway, and the standing stones at Calanais (Callanish). There is a tearoom and shop at Calanais. If you are cycling between Calanais or Carloway and Stornoway, you should note that there is a useful back road, still with a good surface, running north of the A858. This is more direct and very quiet (highlighted on map).

Try to see the broch at Carloway, which is particularly well-preserved. Brochs are something unique to Scotland. They are impregnable towers, usually near the sea. There are brochs all over Scotland but none elsewhere. Built from 100 BC to AD 100, the precise reason for their construction is a mystery. At Arnol is the Black House Museum. This display of how things used to be was actually inhabited up to 1964. North again is

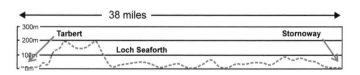

Eoropie, the most northerly village in the Hebrides. The twelfth-century church of St Moluag is here. A key to it is in the shop. A mile north again, the road ends at the Butt of Lewis lighthouse.

Stornoway, the largest town in the Outer Hebrides, is the centre of Scottish Gaelic culture. Caledonian MacBrayne ferries sail from here to Ullapool (2.6 hours). It has hotels, restaurants, B&Bs, hostels and shops, plus a tourist office.

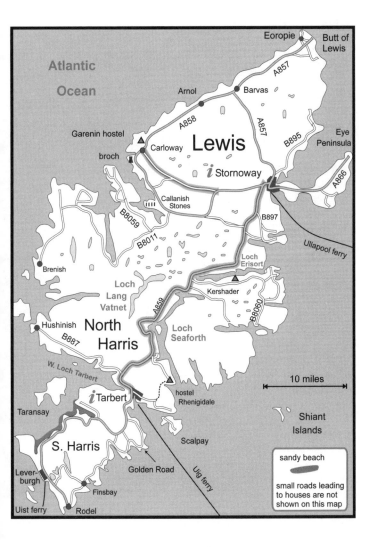

ORKNEY AND SHETLAND

DISTANCES AND ROUTE GRADING

CHAPTER 7

ORKNEY AND SHETLAND

An introduction to cycling on the Orkney Islands is given on page 182. The introduction for Shetland is on page 194. Information on ferry services and accommodation is in the appendix.

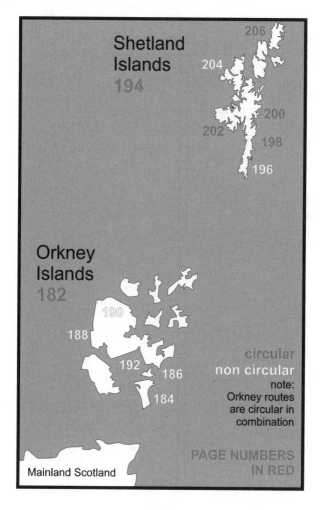

ORKNEY ISLANDS – INTRODUCTION

Most of the roads will be surprisingly quiet, many
historic things to see
Route grading: **mostly Easy**

Orkney consists of a group of over 70 islands and skerries but
only about 20 are inhabited. Mainland (Orkney Mainland)
comprises half of the land area of Orkney. The next largest
island is Hoy, but the cycling is a bit limited on Hoy.

Whatever your taste, you are likely to find something to
interest you in Orkney: the dramatic hills and sea cliffs of
Hoy; the birds, such as puffins, arctic skuas, kittiwakes and
guillemots, to name just a few. Most intriguing is the mystery
of Skara Brae and the Ring of Brodgar: Neolithic
monuments which pre-date the pyramids. The Stromness to
Birsay route takes in the most impressive monuments, and if
you have only one day in Orkney, this might be your top
priority.

The cycling is fairly easy, with no serious hills except in
Hoy. Because of the northern latitude, there will be long hours
of daylight in summer and it can be quite warm. Bear in mind,
however, that there is very little shelter in Orkney because
there are few trees. If you get some rainy days (Atlantic
depressions can still occur in summer), you will need
waterproof clothing.

The routes described take in part of the multi-country
North Sea Cycle Route and the National Cycle Network, and
are signed as 'Route 1' with blue cycle signs. There is no
reason to restrict yourself to these only, however.

One of the pleasures of cycling on islands is island-hopping,
so if you are on Orkney for any length of time you should visit
the smaller islands such as Rousay (a short hop from Tingwall)
or Sanday (great beaches).

Hoy (high island) has some stunning cliff scenery, including
of course the Old Man of Hoy, an impressive rock stack on the
west coast. There are only about 30 miles of road on Hoy, the
most attractive being in the north. Hoy might be an attractive
day trip from Stromness, possibly combining a short cycle ride
with a walk to look at the cliff scenery.

There are ferry services to Orkney from Scrabster on the
Scottish mainland several times a day. There is also a foot

passenger ferry (which takes bikes) from John o' Groats, plus a ferry between Aberdeen, Orkney and Shetland. For more details, see the Appendix.

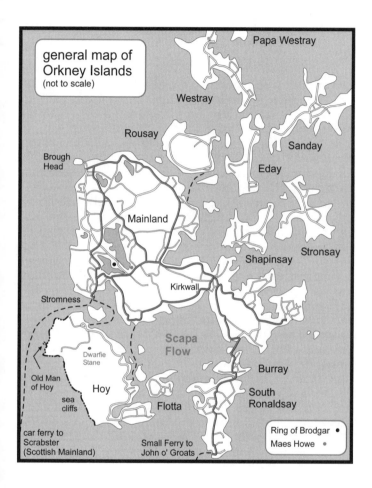

general map of
Orkney Islands
(not to scale)

Papa Westray

Westray

Rousay

Sanday

Brough
Head

Eday

Mainland

Stronsay

Shapinsay

Kirkwall

Stromness

Scapa
Flow

Dwarfie
Stane

Burray

Old Man
of Hoy

Hoy

South
Ronaldsay

sea
cliffs

Flotta

car ferry to
Scrabster
(Scottish Mainland)

Small Ferry to
John o' Groats

Ring of Brodgar •
Maes Howe ·

ORKNEY ISLANDS – SOUTH RONALDSAY

A great cycle route, with views of Scapa Flow and its
eastern approaches
Route grading: **Easy** (9 miles)

Burwick, on the southern tip of the island of South Ronaldsay,
is the starting point of many cycling adventures in Orkney.
The foot passenger ferry from John o' Groats (April to
October), which takes bikes, berths at Burwick.

Just outside the terminal area is a sign for the Tomb of the
Eagles (B9041), an ancient burial site dating from 3000 BC. It
was uncovered by local farmer Ronnie Simison, and is still cared
for by the family. The chambered cairn is in a spectacular cliff-
top setting, and there is a new visitor centre – well worth a visit.

From this site, head back downhill towards the Burwick
terminal junction, and turn right, heading north (A961). The
road carries you up the fairly steep Sandy Hill to the Olad
viewpoint at the top. A nice downhill now past the phone box
on your right leads onto a moderate climb before rolling down
into St Margaret's Hope.

This pretty village, once a herring port, offers local
amenities, accommodation, local craft workshops and
galleries. There is a pleasant square and pier-front area, good
for relaxing for a while. If you feel like some extra miles here,
continue through the square, up past the school and on to
Hoxa Head, where there are good views across Scapa Flow.
There is a sandy beach near Quindry.

Back to St Margaret's Hope and on to Burray. An easy cycle
of around 3 miles takes you over Churchill Barrier No. 4. The
Churchill Barriers were built during the Second World War to
protect the fleet at anchor in Scapa Flow and to link the South
Isles in a defensive chain.

South Ronaldsay is the nearest island to the Scottish
mainland and was the traditional crossing point to Orkney in
times past. The island is 12 kilometres from north to south;
the east coast is rocky, while on the west a long headland

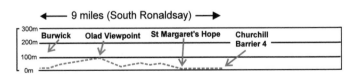

encloses the beautiful sheltered expanse of Widewall Bay.

The village of St Margaret's Hope is named after the bay in which it lies. Traditionally, this is named after Margaret, the seven-year-old Maid of Norway. She was heir to the Scottish throne and died here in 1290 on her way to marry the future Edward II of England. Her early death was an important factor in the Scottish wars of independence.

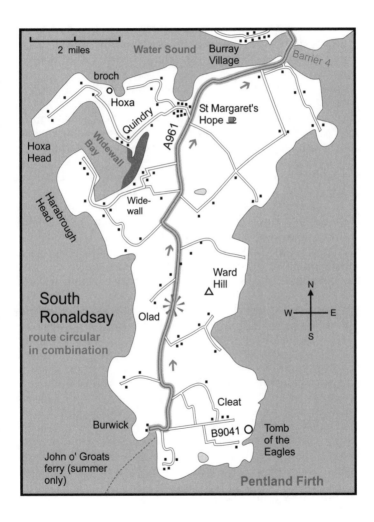

ORKNEY ISLANDS – CHURCHILL BARRIER 4 TO KIRKWALL

A sweep through rolling hills into Orkney's capital, Kirkwall
Route grading: **Easy** (9 miles)

From South Ronaldsay, continue north to Burray. A cycle of three miles from St Margaret's Hope takes you over Barrier No. 4.

Just above the Echna Loch in Burray is the Fossil Centre, which has a café. Up around the corner, head for Barrier No. 3 and across Glims Holm to Barrier No. 2 and the Italian Chapel, on Lamb Holm. Construction of the Barriers was completed in 1945, with help from Italian prisoners of war who transformed one of their Nissen huts into a place of worship. The Chapel is on the right just before Barrier No. 1. Crossing the last Barrier takes you on to St Mary's village, in the Parish of Holm.

A rolling ride past Holm and Gaitnip brings you to Scapa Bay and into Kirkwall. A mile out of the village, you start to climb up to Gutterpool and round to the Holm Straights. There are fine views across the island to the west and north, including across to Kirkwall.

Coming down the hill into Kirkwall, the Highland Park distillery is first on your right. Follow the road downhill into the town centre (A963), go straight ahead at the roundabout, and you will see a cycle shop on your right. Carrying on past the library on your left, take the next right along Castle Street, into central Kirkwall, where you will see St Magnus Cathedral, the Earl's and Bishop's Palaces, and the Orkney Museum (Tankerness House).

On 14 October 1939, the German submarine *U47* slipped through Kirk Sound and torpedoed the battleship HMS *Royal Oak* – 834 men died. Sealing the defences became top priority and work began on the barriers. Italian prisoners of war were used for much of the work but, according to the Geneva Convention, they could not be used for war work, so the

← 9 miles (Burray & Orkney Mainland) →

300m	Churchill	St Mary's
200m	Barrier 4	
100m	Burray Village	Kirkwall
0m		

barriers were designated causeways providing road links to the southern isles.

Camp 60 on Lamb Holm was for much of the war the home of 550 Italian prisoners of war. The Italians were given permission to convert two Nissen huts into a chapel and this became an extraordinary display of artistry. Do not cycle past without visiting it.

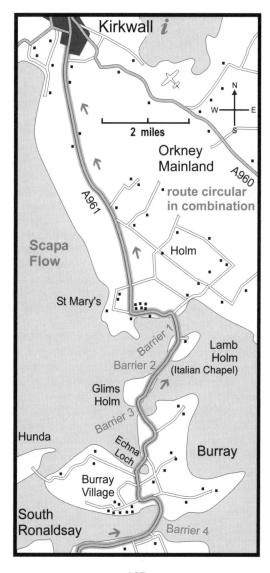

ORKNEY ISLANDS – KIRKWALL TO STROMNESS (VIA ORPHIR)

Sweeping views of Hoy and the anchorage at Stromness
Route grading: **Easy** (19 miles)

Start going south, along Junction Road in central Kirkwall. Pass the library on your right and keep straight on at the roundabout. 300 metres on, take the next right turn to Orphir (A964) and you're heading out towards Scapa Flow. About a mile out of town, the road climbs, passing a garage.

There are views down Scapa Flow as you make your way down to attractive Waulkmill Bay. Pass the nature reserve at Hobbister. If you turn left at Waulkmill and take the single track road for a little way, it will take you down to a magnificent tidal expanse of sand and marsh.

Back on the road, you meet the village of Orphir. Take the road marked 'Gyre' on the left, just after the school. St Nicholas Round Kirk and the Orkneying Saga Centre have an interpretive display, which explains the Norse history of the area. Half a mile further along, you come onto the main road again and on to Houton Bay. The road climbs steeply from here around the Hill of Midland. There are views down Hoy Sound and to Stromness.

From here, it's an easy run along into Stenness, where a left turn to Stromness (A965) passes over the Bridge of Waithe. Take the next left turn and head uphill past the farm of Howe. At the junction with the Ferry Road, turn left towards the town centre. Stromness has B&Bs, hotels and other services.

To the south of Mainland Orkney lies an expanse of water with islands strewn around it. The openings are to the south and previously to the east. Scapa Flow has long been a safe haven. Today it provides a safe berth for oil tankers. During two world wars, Scapa Flow put Orkney at the centre of world history. Scapa Flow became the base for the British battle fleet, the primary purpose of which was to prevent German war ships gaining access to the Atlantic Ocean.

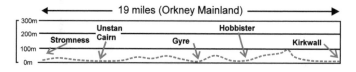

Scapa Flow was also the internment centre for the German High Seas Fleet when it was surrendered at the end of the First World War. It was scuttled there and many of the sunken warships are now a Mecca for recreational divers.

At Hobbister, a bird reserve lies on either side of the road. Houton is a departure point for the ferry to Hoy. This could be one leg of a circular island hop to Hoy, the other being the Stromness–Hoy ferry.

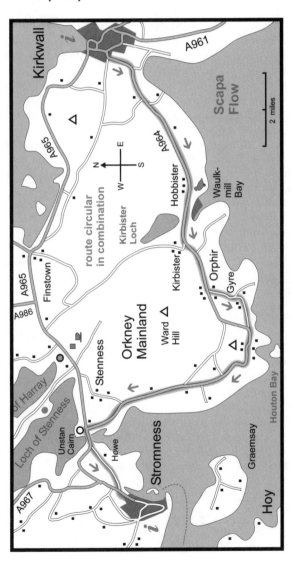

ORKNEY ISLANDS – STROMNESS TO BIRSAY

A cycle through time and history
Route grading: **Easy** (20 miles)

From Stromness, go north past the swimming pool on the road to Kirkwall (A965). A slight diversion past the Bridge of Waithe is to Unstan Chambered Cairn. This gives its name to the Neolithic pottery known as Unstan Ware. Go back to the main road and turn left towards Kirkwall to Tormiston Mill (tearoom). From here, you can walk across the road to Maes Howe, a magnificent 5,000-year-old burial chamber, with Viking runic graffiti.

Head back towards Stromness and turn right at signs for Ring of Brodgar (B9055). On your right are the Standing Stones of Stenness and the Barnhouse Neolithic settlement. Another mile along the loch side is the Ring of Brodgar. Follow this road uphill, and cross the main road, following signs for Skara Brae.

Follow these signs to the Bay of Skaill (B9056), then to Skara Brae and Skaill House. From here, carry on north towards Birsay, through the hills of Marwick. Into the village in Birsay there is St Magnus Kirk and the Earl's Palace to visit. Along a single track road beyond the village is the Brough of Birsay, a tidal island with a Pictish and Norse settlement (accessible at low tide only).

This route takes in some of the most important Neolithic remains in Europe. The chambered tomb at Unstan is near the Bridge of Waithe. It was excavated in 1884 and a large amount of Neolithic pottery was found. Shortly after this is Maes Howe. Despite dating from 2750 BC, it is intact. Maes Howe is a burial chamber. The interior chamber bears Viking graffiti. The Vikings did no damage to the tomb itself. After they left, the tomb remained undisturbed until 1861. The chamber is 4.5 metres square. On the shortest day of the year it is briefly illuminated by the setting sun.

On the way to Skara Brae, you pass the Ring of Brodgar.

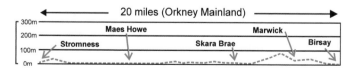

4,700 cubic metres of rock were moved to create it, though what those people believed, and why they did it, is unknown. Before reaching Skara Brae, you pass a minor road leading to Yesnaby. This is an excellent place to see the high cliffs and the power of the Atlantic on a rough day.

Skara Brae is a prehistoric village. Around 45 centuries ago, the village was overwhelmed by a sandstorm. It lay there, preserved by the sand, until another severe storm in 1850 caused it to become exposed again. The remains give a unique guide to the lifestyle of the villagers.

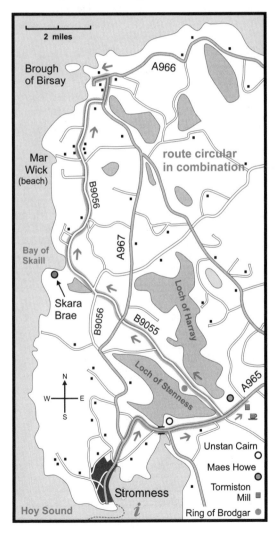

ORKNEY ISLANDS – BIRSAY TO STENNESS (VIA EVIE)

Rugged coastline, panoramic views of the Northern Isles and Maes Howe
Route grading: **Varied** (24 miles)

From Birsay, head east through Swannay and Costa towards Evie (A966). This is quite a hilly section around the coast past Burgar Hill, with the wind turbines on your right. There are views of the island of Eynhallow, which is uninhabited, and across to the Isle of Rousay, the west coast of which has many ancient sites.

In the village of Evie, follow signs to the Broch of Gurness, a partially intact Iron Age broch, and beautiful Aikerness beach. Return back up to the main road, turn left and follow on about 2 miles down the road to Woodwick, where there are gallery/café facilities.

Follow the main road south through Rendall, and take the right turn in the Norseman village to the Lyde Road. This short steep hill takes you into Harray, with beautiful views from the top of Mainland. At the junction with the main road, turn left (A986) and head downhill past the local potter's workshop.

About half a mile further along the main road, turn off right – marked 'Stoneyhill'. This is a rolling ride, with views across the Harray and Stenness Lochs to the hills of Hoy. At the end of this, turn right onto the main road, marked Stromness (A965), as far as Tormiston Mill, almost immediately on your left. From here, you can walk across the road to Maes Howe, a magnificent 5,000-year-old burial chamber, with Viking runic graffiti (see below). From Maes Howe, Kirkwall lies 10 miles to the east, and Stromness 5 miles to the west.

About 500 brochs (which are only found in Scotland) are known to exist, over a fifth of which are in Orkney. The exact purpose of these fortified towers is uncertain, but they are all near the sea and the earliest of them date from around 100 BC.

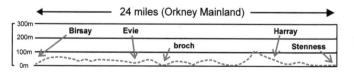

One theory is that they were a defence against Roman slave ships. At that time, England was occupied by the Roman Empire, but the Romans did not succeed in conquering the Picts further north. The Broch of Gurness is one of the best-preserved, and there are also extensive remains of the village that once surrounded it.

Maes Howe is possibly the finest surviving achievement of Neolithic Europe. Despite dating from 2750 BC, it is intact. Maes Howe is a burial chamber, although no bodies were found inside it. The Vikings possibly cleared it out during the twelfth century. The interior chamber bears Viking graffiti – pictures of a serpent and a walrus – plus a number of runes. The Vikings removed treasure, the runes say, but did no damage to the tomb itself. After they left, the tomb remained undisturbed until 1861. The chamber is 4.5 metres square. On the shortest day of the year the chamber is briefly illuminated by the setting sun.

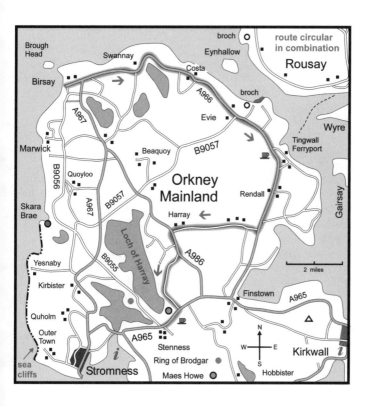

SHETLAND ISLANDS – INTRODUCTION

Long hours of summer daylight, many interesting things
to see
Route grading: **Varied**

There are over 100 islands in Shetland, stretching over 100
kilometres of the Atlantic. There are over 1,000 miles of road,
too, so it's an interesting cycling destination. It's difficult to get
far from the sea. Everywhere there are long sea lochs or voes
and long ridges. The cycle routes here are designed to help
you explore the most interesting parts of the islands.

Shetland is also part of the North Sea Cycle Route. This is
a long distance bike route in Scotland, England, Norway,
Sweden, Germany and the Netherlands. This is now
signposted in Shetland and could be useful to link up many of
the routes described here, which occassionally do touch on
this larger route.

Shetland was ruled from Norway from the ninth century
until 1472, when it was transferred to Scotland. This long
period of Viking domination is reflected in many of the place
names. During the tenth century, the Vikings adopted
Christianity and stopped placing gravegoods in their burial
chambers but, despite this, quite a number of Viking artefacts
can be seen in the Shetland Museum.

Shetland doesn't have the same number of outstanding
prehistoric remains as Orkney – the building stone is less
suitable – but there are still many interesting things to see. For
instance, houses and tombs still survive, which give an insight
into a way of life that existed here up to 5,000 years ago.

There are plenty of roadside telephones and toilets around
the islands and a huge choice of accommodation, ranging from
böds (camping barns), or a youth hostel in Lerwick, through
numerous B&Bs, to luxury hotels. There is a bike shop in
Lerwick, which also does cycle hire.

As in Orkney, there are very few trees so cycling can be
quite exposed – proper waterproof clothing is advised. The
volume of traffic is reasonably low, even on many of the main
roads, so this makes cycling a pleasure. One hazard in the
spring is lambing time. You can be sure that if a lamb and its
mother are on opposite sides of the road, the lamb is going to
run in front of you as you approach!

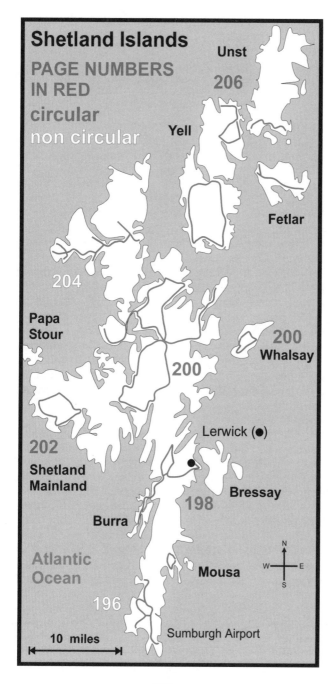

Shetland Islands

PAGE NUMBERS
IN RED
circular
non circular

Unst

206

Yell

Fetlar

204

Papa
Stour

200

Whalsay

200

Lerwick (●)

202

Shetland
Mainland

Bressay

198

Burra

Atlantic
Ocean

Mousa

N
W   E
S

196

Sumburgh Airport

10 miles

SHETLAND ISLANDS – SOUTH MAINLAND

Interesting parts of this long leg of Shetland
Route grading: **Varied** (14 miles)

There are two suggestions here. Both can be linked with the
signposted North Sea Cycle Route. The hills here are covered
with peat moorland. There are fine views of the meadows,
cliffs and sandy beaches along the coast.

BIGTON TO SUMBURGH (LINEAR OR CIRCULAR)

Start at Bigton post office, near the access point for St Ninian's
Isle. Go south on the B9122, then right to a minor road in
Scousburgh. Cycle round Loch Spiggie (bird reserve). You pass
Spiggie Lodge and Hotel. In Ringasta you can turn left to go to
the A970 to continue south, or turn right to Quendale, where a
rough track leads down to the sandy beach. Visit Quendale Mill
here (a restored water mill).

To continue south, cross the A970 at a staggered junction
(left then right). A minor road leads to the Voe inlet and the
village of Boddam. You can either loop north to return to
Bigton via the B9122 to the east of Loch Spiggie, or loop
south to rejoin the A970, which leads eventually to Sumburgh.
The southern loop passes the remains of a broch and Shetland
Croft House Museum.

South of this, the route is the same as the North Sea Cycle
Route and you should follow these signs. On the way, you can
look at Jarlshof, a prehistoric site with Pictish, Viking and
sixteenth-century remains. South of this is the RSPB visitor
centre and Sumburgh Head lighthouse, built by Robert
Stevenson (grandfather of the author Robert Louis Stevenson)
in 1820.

SANDWICK (CIRCULAR, SHORT AND EASY)

Start from Leebitton Pier, which is also the starting point for
the ferry to Mousa (a famous broch). From the pier, go south to

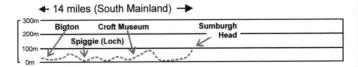

← 14 miles (South Mainland) →

the village of Sandwick. The road then curves round to the north-west, leading to Stove (turn left at the T junction). Continue on to Hoswick, which has a visitor centre. To return to the pier, turn left in Stove towards the A970 but bear right for South Leebitton just before the main road.

Loch Spiggie ('spigg' is Swedish for stickleback) is a good fishing loch and an RSPB bird reserve; hundreds of whooper swans gather here in the autumn.

The Shetland Croft Museum is a complex of several buildings dating from the nineteenth century. The aim is to give a picture of rural life in Shetland a hundred years ago. It includes a house, a byre and a corn mill.

Jarlshof is a prehistoric site with Pictish, Viking and later remains. The site was occupied for 2,500 years prior to the arrival of the Vikings. South of Jarlshof, you can see Sumburgh Head lighthouse. The keeper's accommodation has been taken over by the RSPB. There is a large colony of puffins nearby.

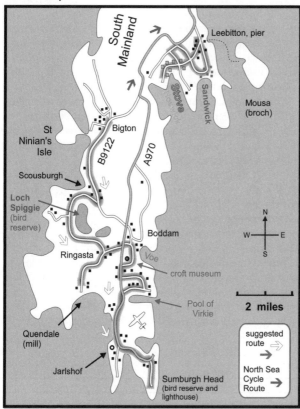

SHETLAND ISLANDS – LERWICK TO WEST BURRA

A partly circular route starting in Shetland's capital
Route grading: **Hilly** (28 miles)

This is an attractive route but the northern circular part is probably not suitable for children, as the area around Lerwick will have quite a lot of traffic. The start of the route is very hilly.

Start at the Lerwick tourist office in Market Cross and travel south on the A970 for a mile to a roundabout. Turn right to North Clickimin Centre Campsite, then follow a track climbing steeply up Staney Hill. This becomes Ladies Drive. Turn left, pass some radio masts, then descend to the A970, where you turn left.

At Bridge of Fitch, you can go to the B9074 then via Tingwall (3 extra miles), or continue south on the A970. Continuing south after two more miles, there's a great view of West and East Burra, then you descend steeply towards Scalloway. Turn left just before Scalloway (castle) to the B9074.

Continue south on the B9074. Just before entering Hamnavoe, turn left for West Burra. The road eventually runs out just over a mile before the southern tip of West Burra. There is a footpath but it doesn't go all the way. There are food shops at Bridge End and Hamnavoe.

Return by the way you came to Scalloway, but a mile after that, fork right onto the B9073. Apart from the West Burra leg, most of the route is part of the North Sea Cycle Route.

Two prominent features of the Loch of Clickimin at the start of the route are a broch and a longhouse. The water level used to be higher here, and the broch was originally on an islet. Some interesting things were found there, including a Roman glass bowl made in Egypt around AD 100 (the site is maintained by Historic Scotland).

Just south of Tingwall (if you go that way), at the head of the loch, you will pass an information board for Law Ting

28 miles (30 via Tingwall) Central Mainland (part circular)

300m	Lerwick		Scalloway	Hamnavoe junction		Scalloway	B9073	Lerwick
200m	Bridge of Fitch			Burra road end				
100m			outward			return		
0m								

Holm, a Viking assembly place. There are standing stones at the south end of the loch, near the golf course.

Scalloway has shops and pubs, as well as quite a lot of interesting buildings in various states of ruin. This might be a good place for a pub lunch but, after that, certainly have a look at the castle. If you have time, the stately house of Old Ha is worth seeing. The central part of Scalloway is a place of winding streets and old buildings with great atmosphere, so spend a little time wandering around.

The three islands of East and West Burra and Trondra once had a large fishing community but this is much reduced. Trondra is green and empty but North and East Burra are more populated, with low cliffs and some attractive beaches.

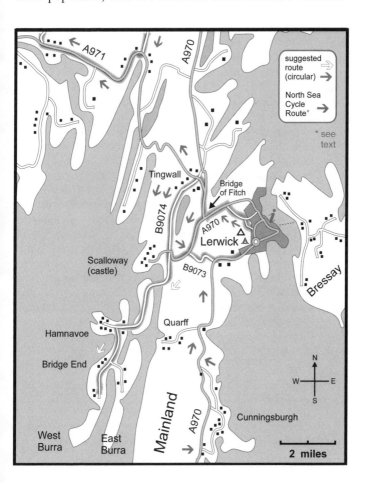

SHETLAND ISLANDS – CENTRAL MAINLAND AND WHALSAY

Two different circular options, starting from Voe
Route grading: **Hilly** (22 or 25 miles)

This route is basically a northern and a southern loop, starting from Voe, plus two possible additions at Lunna Ness and Whalsay. You might do one loop in the morning, the other in the afternoon, and have lunch at Voe. The northern part includes the oil terminal at Sullom Voe. There will be a certain amount of traffic on the A970, and if you are cycling with children, you might prefer to restrict yourself to Whalsay and the Lunna Ness peninsula (see map, opposite).

This part of Mainland contains the largest area of high ground in Shetland, and the Mainland loops tend to be hilly at times. The B9071 south of Voe has steep hills but there are good views towards Muckle Roe.

Lunna Ness and Whalsay are much less hilly. Cycling out on the Lunna Ness peninsula will give good views of the southern tip of Yell. Whalsay would be a good option if you want a short cycle ride with a ferry trip.

Much of the time you will find yourself cycling by the coast. There is a lot of attractive scenery – don't be put off by the oil terminal. The narrow neck of land, interestingly called Mavis Grind, which separates Sullom Voe from St Magnus Bay, is sometimes described as separating the Atlantic from the North Sea.

Whalsay, it is sometimes said, is Shetland in miniature, and if you have only a limited time and want a short cycle ride, this would be a good option. The harbour at Symbister combines

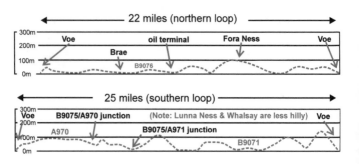

modern buildings with restored sixteenth-century dwellings. There is a sandy beach near the village of Sandwick in the south.

On Mainland, Voe is an attractive small village with a Norwegian feel to it. It has little wooden houses nestling around the pier, and what looks remarkably like a fjord. Brae, five miles further north, isn't quite so attractive.

The road on the southern section just east of Tresta rises to 114 metres from sea level and offers a great view of the two narrow peninsulas of Strom Ness and White Ness to the south.

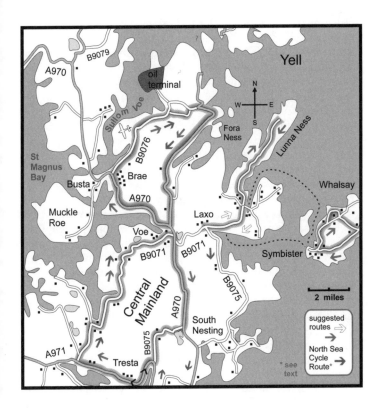

SHETLAND ISLANDS – WEST MAINLAND

Two different circular options, starting from Voe
Route grading: **Varied** (14 miles)

This is one of the prettiest areas of Shetland, with little lochans and islets scattered about. It also has an excellent network of quiet rural roads so is one of the best areas for cycling. As well as sheep, you will see herds of Shetland ponies, though by mid-summer, sheep and ponies might look a bit scruffy, as both will be losing their coats. Walls is the main centre and would be a good base for exploring.

At one time, Walls was an important fishing centre but, in common with a great many other places, this has declined. There are several prehistoric remains around the Walls area, which you are likely to come across. We know very little about the ancient people who lived here around 1600 BC and the associated explanations are partly informed guesswork.

The suggested route here takes you west out of Walls, past Burrastow House Hotel, then on to Mid Walls and Dale. At Dale, there is an option of taking a short walk (about a mile) to the Voe of Dale. After this, the route goes north-east to join the A971, where you turn right to go south-east. Near Bridge of Walls, you can look at the prehistoric settlement of Scord of Brouster. This is one of the most complete Neolithic settlement complexes in Shetland, and recent excavations and radiocarbon dating have yielded some valuable results.

The other minor roads in West Mainland are well worth exploring. The area around Skeld is very quiet and has good views towards South Mainland and West and East Burra. Another option would be to bike north to West Burrafirth. From here, you can take a ferry to Papa Stour but this only has a couple of miles of road.

Apart from the attractive scenery, some of the most interesting things in this area are the prehistoric remains. The best of these is the Scord of Brouster settlement near Bridge of Walls. The extent of this settlement, which contains many

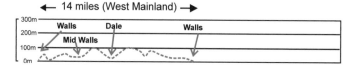

houses together with a temple, has assisted archaeologists in making sense of the site as a whole. Generally, the site dates from the third millennium BC, but it was occupied for a very long period and radiocarbon dating suggests that parts of it have been occupied for over one and a half thousand years. The climate of Shetland was rather warmer at this time.

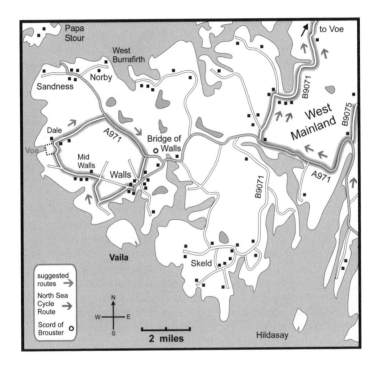

SHETLAND ISLANDS – NORTH MAINLAND

Two different circular options starting from Voe
Route grading: **Hilly** (13 + 3 miles)

North Mainland has dramatic scenery, including Ronas Voe, the only real fjord in Shetland. Other attractions include a wildlife sanctuary, and the prominent Ronas Hill, as well as cliffs at Eshaness. Accommodation can be found at the camping böd at Hamnavoe.

You might be tempted to go up to North Roe but in fact the best scenery is between Ollaberry and Eshaness in the centre. You get a good view of the high cliffs of Ronas Voe from the minor road on the south side. A look at this could be combined with a trip up Collafirth Hill and to Ollaberry. Going to Ollaberry is pretty hilly too. It would be possible to extend this trip by walking a further two miles to Ronas Hill, the highest point in Shetland.

If you are heading towards Eshaness, a good place to start would be the St Magnus Hotel in Hillswick (at the end of the A970). The Booth Wildlife Sanctuary is near here. Going west along the B9078, you have a number of choices. There is a museum in Tangwick Haa. This is a typical example of a laird's house dating from the seventeenth century.

Near the furthest point west of Eshaness, there's the Broch and Hole of Scraada. These two things are unconnected and are a little way apart. The hole is a natural feature and the broch is the remains of a fortified tower (not impressive). Near too is the lighthouse at South Head.

Hillswick was developed as a fishing station during the nineteenth century. The local St Magnus Bay Hotel was built of Scots pine in Norway and re-erected in Hillswick at the beginning of the twentieth century. It was the Shetland terminal of the old North of Scotland Shipping Company.

Ronas Hill at 450 metres is the highest point in Shetland. It has a watchtower and on a clear day offers great views of all the groups of islands.

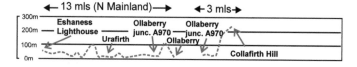

The coast at Eshaness comprises cliffs, stacks and arches where the sea, cutting into faults, has created unusual features. This is a great place for seeing guillemot, puffins, fulmars and other sea birds.

As well as Johnnie Notion's camping böd, Hamnavoe also has a great pebble beach, where winter storms have driven the pebbles to 18 metres high. You won't meet Johnnie, however, as he was born in 1740. He became the local weaver, blacksmith, clock repairer, joiner and bone-setter. He was also more successful in dealing with smallpox than the local doctors.

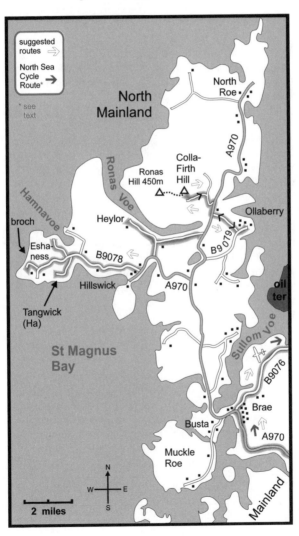

SHETLAND ISLANDS – YELL AND UNST

John o' Groats has nothing on this
Route grading: **Varied** (13 + 3 miles)

Yell is less populated than Unst, though it is a necessary step on the way to Unst. Mostly it consists of moorland, but as the road generally follows the coast, there is still plenty of variety. The ferries to Fetlar and Unst are from the north of Yell, departing from Gutcher pier. Interesting features on Yell include the Old Ha Visitor Centre at Burravoe, a beautifully solid whitewashed building. Just east of Mid Yell is the aptly named Windhouse, the ruin of a mansion built in 1707. Its lodge beside the road has been restored and is now a camping böd.

Fetlar is different from most of the Shetland islands in that it lacks a safe harbour. It is attractive to bird-watchers, as there are a number of rare species (and there is an RSPB hide here). There are a number of broch sites, though none of them is as complete as the Broch of Mousa. A more recent ruin is Brough Lodge; built in the 1820s for the island laird Sir Arthur Nicholson, its grand pretensions are best viewed from a safe distance.

Unst is the most northerly island of Scotland; John o' Groats has nothing on this. The lighthouse Muckle Flugga is on an outlying skerry (rocky islet). This was possibly the most difficult of all British lighthouse-building projects. A look at the lighthouse will involve a six-mile walk.

Possibly a more realistic Unst cycling journey for you would be from the Belmont ferry terminal to Muness, which has a castle. On the way, you can see standing stones and visit a knitwear factory. If this seems a little mundane, by all means wander further north. Unst is a surprisingly green and populated island.

While opinions differ about the attractiveness of Yell, (the name means barren) it certainly has a great camping böd in the renovated gatehouse lodge of Windhouse just east of Mid Yell. The village of Cullievoe in the north of Yell is worth visiting. There is an attractive beach a couple of miles further north at

Breckon. There is also an attractive beach further south at West Sandwick.

Unst is reputed to mean 'eagle isle' and indeed sea eagles did breed there at one time. Baltasound is the name of the major settlement on Unst, as well as the sound on which it stands. There is an oil-rig supply base there and it is the export port for talc, which is mined further north near Haroldswick. Apparently, most of it goes for roofing felt, rather than for sprinkling on yourself.

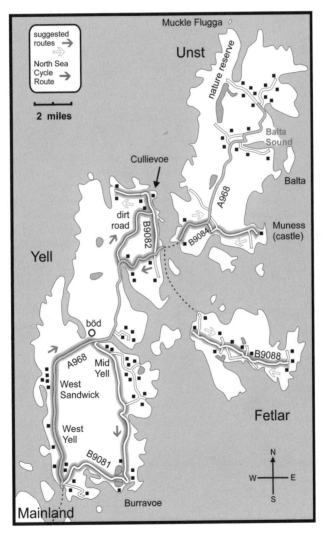

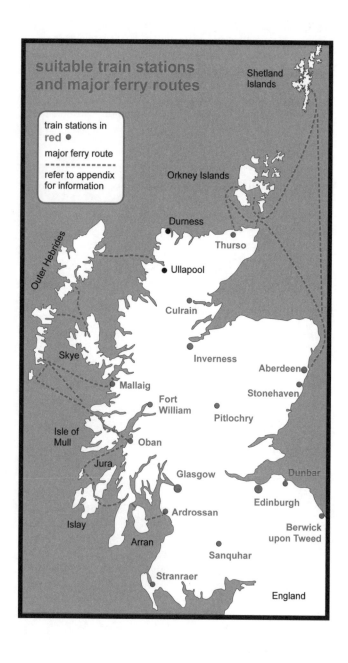

suitable train stations
and major ferry routes

Shetland
Islands

train stations in
red ●

major ferry route
- - - - - - - - - - - -
refer to appendix
for information

Orkney Islands

Outer Hebrides

Durness

Thurso

Ullapool

Culrain

Skye

Inverness

Aberdeen

Stonehaven

Mallaig

Fort
William

Pitlochry

Isle of
Mull

Oban

Jura

Glasgow

Dunbar

Edinburgh

Islay

Ardrossan

Arran

Berwick
upon Tweed

Sanquhar

Stranraer

England

APPENDIX

WHERE TO STAY AND HOW TO GET THERE!

It isn't difficult to find transport information: the various telephone numbers and website addresses are given here. Finding a place to lay your head can be more of a problem. This is particularly so if you are on a bicycle, in some out of the way place, and need to keep to your budget.

Currently, I find the internet frustrating because every accommodation website claims to have B&Bs virtually everywhere. When you look in detail, you find it's 20 miles up some busy road – not very convenient on a bike!

The Scottish Area Tourist Boards nowadays tend to answer calls from call centres. However efficient this may be, it also means that the person you speak to may lack local knowledge.

Fortunately, there is a good alternative – the local Tourist Information Centre (TIC). These local offices (*i* symbol on maps) are staffed by people who usually have an intimate knowledge of their own area. Don't forget to mention you are on a bicycle. For more general information, contact Visit Scotland, see below.

The telephone numbers and addresses of the relevant Scottish TICs are given on the following pages. Of course, it is best to do your research and book ahead before you begin your journey. Bear in mind that many of the TICs will be shut in the winter. Unlike the call centres, they may be closed in the evening.

Finally, I should mention that, while trains in Scotland do carry bicycles, they don't carry large numbers of them. Once you have bought your train ticket, you can also reserve a bike space. Often this is free, and you can do it by phone or over the internet. Buses don't usually carry bicycles, although some drivers may oblige, particularly in the Outer Hebrides for some reason. All ferries take bikes.

CYCLE HIRE

You can rent mountain bikes in very many places in Scotland, but the following shops offer a wide range of cycles. Tourist Information Centres should also be able to put you in touch with cycle-hirers (see following pages).

Dales Cycles
Dobbies Loan
Glasgow G3 0JE
0141 332 2705

Bike Trax Cycle Hire
13 Lochrin Place
Edinburgh EH3 9QX
0131 228 6633

Edinburgh Cycle Hire
29 Blackfriars Street
Edinburgh EH1 1NB
0131 556 5560

PUBLIC TRANSPORT

Trains: For train information, phone 0845 484950. If you are using the train to plan a long cycle trip, it is advisable to book a bike space well in advance.

For information on cycle carriage on Scotrail trains, see www.scotrail.co.uk/cycle.htm.

For GNER trains, phone 08457 225225, or see www.gner.co.uk/pages/bikes.html.

For Virgin trains, contact the customer helpline on 08457 222333, or email customer.relations@virgintrains.co.uk.

Buses in Scotland do not generally carry bikes, unless they are partly taken apart and contained in a bike box. Sometimes in rural areas drivers may oblige, but you cannot rely on this. Bus drivers in the Outer Hebrides will usually carry bikes.

SUSTRANS

Sustrans – it stands for sustainable transport – is a charity that works on practical projects to encourage people to walk, cycle and use public transport in order to reduce motor traffic and its adverse effects.

APPENDIX

Sustrans
National Cycle Network Centre
2 Cathedral Square
Bristol
BS1 5DD
0845 113 0065
www.nationalcyclenetwork.org.uk

Sustrans Scotland (address due to change in June 2004)
162 Fountainbridge
Edinburgh EH3 7AA
0131 624 7660

OTHER USEFUL ADDRESSES

P&O Scottish Ferries
Jamieson's Quay
Aberdeen AB10 1YL
(Orkney and Shetland)
01224 288800

John o' Groats Ferries
John o' Groats KW1 4YR
(foot and bicycle ferry to Orkney)
01955 611353

Caledonian MacBrayne
Hebridean & Clyde Ferries
The Ferry Terminal
Gourock 0990 650000
www.calmac.co.uk

Spokes
Lothian Cycle Campaign
232 Dalry Road
Edinburgh EH11 2JG
0131 313 2114
www.spokes.org.uk

Scottish Youth Hostels Association
7 Glebe Crescent
Stirling FK8 2JA
01786 891400
www.syha.org.uk

Visit Scotland
23 Ravelston Terrace
Edinburgh EH4 3EU
0131 332 2433
www.cycling.visitscotland.com

Fife Millennium Cycle Ways
Fife House
North Street
Glenrothes KY7 5LT
01592 413043
www.fife-cycleways.co.uk

SELECTED TOURIST INFORMATION CENTRES

These are indicated on the maps with a red *i* symbol. Some of those listed are off-map but may be useful. Please note that these centres are often manned by a single person, and may be closed in the evenings.

Aberdeen
23 Union Street
Aberdeen
AB11 5BP
Tel: 01224 288828
Jan–Dec

Aberfeldy
The Square
Aberfeldy PH15 2DD
Tel: 01887 820276
Jan–Dec

Aberfoyle
Trossachs Discovery Centre
Main Street
Aberfoyle FK8 3UQ
Tel: 08707 200604
Jan–Dec

Anstruther
Scottish Fisheries Museum
Harbourhead
Anstruther KY10 3AB
Tel: 01333 311073
Apr–Oct

Auchterarder
90 High Street
Auchterarder PH3 1BJ
Tel: 01764 663450
Jan–Dec

Aviemore
Grampian Road
Aviemore PH22 1PP
Tel: 01479 810363
Jan–Dec

Ballater
Albert Hall
Station Square
Ballater AB35 5QB
Tel: 013397 55306
Jan–Dec

Balloch
The Old Station Building
Balloch G83 8LQ
Tel: 08707 200607
Apr–Oct

Banchory
Bridge Street
Banchory AB31 3SX
Tel: 01330 822000
Easter–Oct

Berwick-upon-Tweed
106 Marygate
Berwick-upon-Tweed
Northumberland TD15 1BN
Tel: 01289 330733
Mar–Sept, Oct–Feb

Biggar
155 High Street
Biggar ML12 6DL
Tel: 01899 221066
Easter–Sep

Blairgowrie
26 Wellmeadow
Blairgowrie PH10 6AS
Tel: 01250 872960
Jan–Dec

Bowmore
Isle of Islay PA43 7JP
Tel: 08707 200617
Jan–Dec

Braemar
The Mews
Mar Road
Braemar AB35 5YP
Tel: 013397 41600
Jan–Dec

Brodick
The Pier
Brodick, Isle of Arran
KA27 8AU
Tel: 01292 678100
Jan–Dec

Callander
Rob Roy Centre, Ancaster Square
Callander FK17 8ED
Tel: 08707 200628
Mar–Dec, and weekends

Castlebay
Main Street
Castlebay, Isle of Barra
HS9 5XD
Tel: 01871 810336
Easter–Oct

Castle Douglas
Market Hill Car Park
Castle Douglas DG7 1AE
Tel: 01556 502611
Easter–Oct

Craignure
The Pier
Craignure, Isle of Mull
PA65 6AY
Tel: 08707 200610
Jan–Dec

Crail
Museum & Heritage Centre
Marketgate
Crail KY10 3TL
Tel: 01333 450859
Apr–Oct

Crieff
High Street
Crieff PH7 3HU
Tel: 01764 652578
Jan–Dec

Daviot Wood Picnic Area, A9
Daviot Wood by Inverness IV1 2ER
Tel: 01463 772203
Apr–Oct

Drumnadrochit
The Car Park
Drumnadrochit
IV63 6TX
Tel: 01456 459076
Easter–Oct

Drymen
The Library
The Square
Drymen G63 0BL
Tel: 08707 200611
May–Sep

Dufftown
Clock Tower
The Square
Dufftown AB55 4AD
Tel: 01340 820501
Easter–Oct

Dumfries
64 Whitesands
Dumfries DG1 2RS
Tel: 01387 253862
Jan–Dec

Dunbar
143A High Street
Dunbar EH42 1ES
Tel: 0845 22 55 121
Apr–Oct

Dundee
21 Castle Street
Dundee DD1 3AA
Tel: 01382 527527
Jan–Dec

Dunfermline
1 High Street
Dunfermline KY12 7DL
Tel: 01383 720999
Apr–Oct

Dunkeld
The Cross
Dunkeld PH8 0AN
Tel: 01350 727688
Apr–Dec

Dunoon
7 Alexandra Parade
Dunoon PA23 8AB
Tel: 08707 200629
Jan–Dec

Dunvegan
2 Lochside
Dunvegan, Isle of Skye IV55 8WB
Tel: 01470 521581
Apr–Oct, limited opening Nov–March

APPENDIX

Durness
Durine
Durness IV27 4PN
Tel: 01971 511259
Jan–Dec, closed weekends Oct–Mar

Edinburgh
Edinburgh & Scotland Information Centre
3 Princes Street
Edinburgh EH2 2QP
Tel: 0845 22 55 121
Jan–Dec

Elgin
17 High Street
Elgin IV30 1EG
Tel: 01343 542666/543388
Jan–Dec

Eyemouth
Auld Kirk
Market Square
Eyemouth TD14 5HE
Tel: 018907 50678
Easter–Oct

Falkirk
2–4 Glebe Street
Falkirk FK1 1HU
Tel: 08707 200614
Jan–Dec

Forfar
45 East High Street
Forfar DD8 2EG
Tel: 01307 467876
Easter–Sep

Forres
116 High Street
Forres IV36 0NP
Tel: 01309 672938
Easter–Oct

Fort Augustus
Car Park
Fort Augustus PH32 4DD
Tel: 01320 366367
Apr–Oct

Fort William
Cameron Centre
Cameron Square
Fort William PH33 6AJ
Tel: 01397 703781
Jan–Dec

Glasgow
11 George Square
Glasgow G2 1DY
Tel: 0141 204 4400
Jan–Dec

Grantown-on-Spey
54 High Street
Grantown-on-Spey PH26 3AS
Tel: 01479 872773
Jan–Nov

Inveraray
Front Street
Inveraray PA32 8UY
Tel: 08707 200616
Jan–Dec

Inverness
Castle Wynd
Inverness IV2 3BJ
Tel: 01463 234353
Jan–Dec

Jedburgh
Murrays Green
Jedburgh TD8 6BE
Tel: 0870 608 0404 (call centre)
Jan–Dec

APPENDIX

Kelso
Town House
The Square
Kelso TD5 7HF
Tel: 0870 608 0404 (call centre)
Jan–Dec

Kilchoan
Pier Road, Kilchoan PH36 4LH
Tel: 01972 510222
Apr–Oct

Killin
Breadalbane Folklore Centre
Main Street
Killin FK21 8XE
Tel: 08707 200627
Mar–Oct

Kirkwall
6 Broad Street
Kirkwall, Orkney
KW15 1DH
Tel: 01856 872856
Jan–Dec

Kirriemuir
Cumberland Close
Kirriemuir DD8 4EF
Tel: 01575 574097
Easter–Sep

Lerwick
The Market Cross
Lerwick, Shetland
ZE1 0LU
Tel: 01595 693434
Jan–Dec

Linlithgow
Burgh Halls
The Cross
Linlithgow EH49 7AH
Tel: 0845 22 55 121
Apr–Oct

Loch Lomond Gateway Centre
Loch Lomond Shores
Balloch G83 8QL
Tel: 08707 200631
Jan–Dec

Lochboisdale
Pier Road
Lochboisdale, Isle of South Uist HS8 5TH
Tel: 01878 700286
Easter–Oct

Lochgilphead
Lochnell Street
Lochgilphead PA31 8JL
Tel: 08707 200618
Apr–Oct

Lochinver
Kirk Lane
Lochinver IV27 4LT
Tel: 01571 844330
Apr–Oct

Lochmaddy
Pier Road
Lochmaddy, Isle of North Uist HS6 5AA
Tel: 01876 500321
Easter–Oct

Mallaig
PH41 4SQ
Tel: 01687 462170
Apr–Oct, limited opening Oct–Mar

Melrose
Abbey House
Abbey Street
Melrose TD6 9LG
Tel: 0870 608 0404 (call centre)
Jan–Dec

Moffat
Unit 1
Ladyknowe
Moffat DG10 9DY
Tel: 01683 220620
Easter–Oct

Montrose
Bridge Street
Montrose DD10 8AB
Tel: 01674 672000
Easter–Sep

Newton Stewart
Bashwood Square
Newton Stewart DG8 6EQ
(no public telephone number)
Mar–Sep, Oct–Feb

North Berwick
Quality Street
North Berwick EH39 4HJ
Tel: 0845 22 55 121
Jan–Dec

Oban
Argyll Square
Oban PA34 4AR
Tel: 08707 200630
Jan–Dec

Penicuik
Edinburgh Crystal Visitor Centre
Penicuik EH26 8HB
Tel: 0845 22 55 121
Easter–Sep

Perth
Lower City Mills
West Mill Street
Perth PH1 5QP
Tel: 01738 450600
Jan–Dec

Pitlochry
22 Atholl Road
Pitlochry PH16 5BX
Tel: 01796 472215/472751
Jan–Dec

Portree
Bayfield House
Portree, Isle of Skye IV51 9EL
Tel: 01478 612137
Jan–Dec

Rothesay
Winter Gardens
Rothesay, Isle of Bute
PA20 0AJ
Tel: 08707 200619
Jan–Dec

St Andrews
70 Market Street
St Andrews KY16 9NU
Tel: 01334 472021
Jan–Dec

Selkirk
Halliwells House
Selkirk TD7 4BL
Tel: 0870 608 0404
Easter–Oct

Stonehaven
66 Allardice Street
Stonehaven AB39 9ET
Tel: 01569 762806
Easter–Oct

Stornoway
26 Cromwell Street
Stornoway, Isle of Lewis HS1 2DD
Tel: 01851 703088
Jan–Dec

Stranraer
28 Harbour Street
Stranraer DG9 7RA
Tel: 01776 702595
Jan–Dec

Stromness
Ferry Terminal Building
Stromness, Pier Head
Orkney KW16 3AA
Tel: 01856 850716
Jan–Dec

Strontian
PH36 4HZ
Tel: 01967 402381
Fax: 01967 402131
Apr–Oct

Tarbert (Harris)
Pier Road
Tarbert, Isle of Harris
HS3 3DG
Tel: 01859 502011
Easter–Oct

Tarbert (Loch Fyne)
Harbour Street
Tarbert PA29 6UD
Tel: 08707 200624
Apr–Oct

Thurso
Riverside
Thurso KW14 8BU
Tel: 01847 892371
Apr–Oct

Tobermory
The Pier
Tobermory
Isle of Mull PA75 6NU
Tel: 08707 200625
Apr–Oct

Tomintoul
The Square
Tomintoul AB37 9ET
Tel: 01807 580285
Fax: 01807 580285
Easter–Oct

Tyndrum
Main Street
Tyndrum FK20 8RY
Tel: 08707 200626
Apr–Oct

Ullapool
Argyle Street
Ullapool IV26 2UB
Tel: 01854 612135
Fax: 01854 613031
Jan–Dec